LOVE ME
WITH ALL OF YOUR HEART
OR LEAVE ME
WITH ALL OF MINE

Clinton D. Williams

ELISHEVA PUBLISHING INC.

Kelowna, British Columbia
Canada

Edited by: wordsharp.net
Cover Design: Navigator Multimedia
Cover Photography: Ashley Siebert, Blissful Visions Photography
Book Design: Jill Veitch, Webb Publishing.ca

Published by Elisheva Publishing Inc.
Kelowna, British Columbia, Canada
ISBN: 978-0-9877850-0-8

A special thanks to Dr. Gordon Neufeld,
who taught me truly how to
understand my children,

to Dr. Warshak, who taught my children
truly how to understand their parents,

and to Ellen DeGeneres for keeping me laughing
and feeling positive through the tough times.

INSIDE

MIDDLE

END

ABOUT THE AUTHOR

Clint Williams is a single parent of two boys. His elder son is thirteen and the younger is three; they each have a different mother, but share him as their father. The stress of the break up was monumental and permanently scarring for his elder son, and now his three-year-old son faces the same situation. Why do children have to be forced through this? The sad truth is that most parents who have split up, or are in the process of splitting up, will not see what their actions are doing to their children.

Clint is not a doctor, child psychologist, nor a counselor; he is a parent who has been alienated for the better part of twelve years. In that time, he has learned from his experiences, as well as his mistakes and has searched for answers. He has found these answers from experience, trial and error, seeking professional help through books, seminars, and videos, as well as meeting with child and adult professionals. He has put an end to his own parent alienation, doing so with a positive drive and sense of humour. He is dedicated to helping others facing similar circumstances.

PROLOGUE

Picture this: You are getting ready to drop your child off at their new daycare. When you arrive, you get out of the vehicle; unbuckle your child from their seat, and head toward the door. Anticipation builds in both of you. When you knock, there's no answer, so you go on in. When you go in, you are startled to hear the daycare worker yelling at a child, punishing a child in an unfair manner. What do you do? You would leave with your child. They may not hurt your child physically, but wouldn't the thought of this kind of verbal and emotional abuse prevent you from leaving your child in their care? Of course it would. However, when we, as parents, generate enough hatred and/or jealousy toward each other we are in fact doing exactly the same thing, making poor choices for our children out of anger toward the other parent. Decisions are never positive nor are they productive when made out of anger.

I am not saying that both parents are always doing the wrong thing. I know that each case is different and you probably think that you are the one doing everything right and they are the ones doing everything wrong. It happens occasionally, rarely, but occasionally. No parent who is doing the wrong things will admit it or even thinks they are doing anything wrong. It is like my bad driver theory.

Look at how many bad drivers are out there, and how much we all complain about them or tell stories about them. We find ourselves swearing at someone when we get cut off and say things like "people like that shouldn't be able to drive." The interesting part is despite so many bad drivers driving out there, have you ever actually talked to one? I have tried to find some to talk to and wouldn't you know it, you can't find a one. People will point out bad drivers but no one admits that they are the bad driver. Bad drivers must come from somewhere! But think about it, when was the last time you heard someone in the lunchroom say, "Oh Sarah, you should have seen how crappy I drove to work today! It was hilarious; I suck. I cut off three people and almost hit a cyclist. I should not be allowed to have a license; they should just take it away!" Then everyone laughs.... Nope, you don't hear such things, just like when you talk to parents individually there are no bad parents out there. Wouldn't it make sense that someone is doing something that is not right? Maybe it is you, or maybe it is them. I don't know. What I do know is this: sometimes it is difficult to see yourself and what you are doing. It would be nice if we could just take out an eyeball and hold it above us to have an objective eye on the situation. A view from above that is clear, and not obscured by our own stubbornness. Perhaps the other person in your life is the grief causer. The point of this book is to help you see what might be really going on. Let me be your objective eye. If you don't admit anything is your fault, read this book closely. If you feel no guilt while reading this book, then you are probably right and you can help others with what you learn. However, if just one thing mentioned in this book resembles you or your actions, you don't need to admit it to anyone, but you need to start making changes. It is not too late to do the right thing, to gain the full love of your children and perhaps even a symbiotic relationship with your ex.

One of the first people I told about my idea for this book was a middle-aged mom who had been through a divorce. She replied, "Most of us have kids and know what the crap is all about, and the ones who don't have kids aren't going to care about a book about people with kids. No one will read your book." Phewwww! Talk about positive motivation to start the book. Well, instead of feeding off the negativity, I pushed ahead with determination. This person had just proved my point of why people need a book like this - to stop this kind of attitude. Change will never happen if we continue to say, "Who cares? It happens all the time and there is nothing we can do about it." There is something we can do about it. We can take a close look at our individual situations and actions, identify the problems, admit what you personally are doing wrong and start making positive changes for the sake of our children who will one day be the generation in charge.

This book is not about bashing parents. Its purpose is to create and make change. Change starts with one simple action that can grow into many others. Change starts with taking the first step.

BEGINNING

1. THE NOTE

I wake up. I don't know or care what time it is. I am excited, I run down the hallway, I don't care if it's messy or if it's small. I want to play. Everyone is still sleeping, so I turn on the cartoons quietly; I don't want to wake them up.

Today is a new day, and it's sooo exciting, so much to do: play with toys, watch cartoons. When Mom and Dad drink their coffee, I can go outside and find that stick I was playing with yesterday. It was a magic stick; I hope nobody found it. I will get dirty and my parents will frown but I don't get it; why should they frown when I am having so much fun? Oooh my bike! I forgot about my bike. I can ride my bike too; my parents sometimes say I go too fast but I don't care; I'm having fun. When my parents do something silly, I remember what they say to me and I say it to them. "You be careful; you don't want to get an owie", they just laugh. Why do they laugh when that's what they say to me?

They get out of bed, and just when I think I'm going to be in trouble, they smile and ask me what I'm watching and then ask why I didn't wake them up. I reply with just a shrug of my shoulders. Breakfast is shoved in front of me but who has time to eat? Now that my parents are up, the door is open, open to the outside, except for this silly rule they made up that I have to eat breakfast before I go play outside. I eat faster than fast, the faster I eat it, then the faster I get to be outside.

I just started playing, there is so much fun to have, and then I get called in for lunch. I just had breakfast! I don't want to eat again; my bike is just about to go through the Super Duper Bike Wash. I turned the hose on all by myself. Harrumph! Now I have to shut off the hose and my bike is GOING TO GET DIRTY, just so I can eat lunch. I grumble on my way in, stomping to show my displeasure but no one sees. So I do what I have to, eat as fast as I can so I can finish my Super Duper Bike Wash. Does anyone see how important this is? If Spencer gets his bike done first, then mine will just be a Bike Wash, nothing super-duper about that!

I finish my lunch; I don't even know what I ate and I get back to my Super Duper Bike Wash. My bike is looking great and everything is perfect, until I hear my parents yell, "Turn off the hose and come inside, you're getting all wet." Duh, of course I am getting wet; this is the Super Duper Bike Wash! So now I have to go inside and change; again I stomp and again my rebellion goes unnoticed.

Now that I am dry and ready to play again it is time to eat supper. Sheesh, I just had lunch! Eating sure gets in the way of playtime. "I'm not hungry." I say again, and again, it didn't work. So I eat as fast as I can and save a few bites so when I say I'm full, I can eat the so important Last Bite! Or eat as many as I am old. I think about what happens to you when you're grandpa's age; when he is full does he still have to eat like a zillion bites? He would blow up; no wonder grandpa always says he's hungry.

So after all that, I am not allowed to go outside again; they called me in because I was getting wet and now I have to jump in the tub. I don't get it but if I do it right away I can still watch some TV. I love TV; cartoons are my favorite.

I wake up the next morning and Mom is crying. Mom says things will be different now because Mommy and Daddy won't live in the same house anymore. I am confused, was my Super Duper Bike Wash that bad?

Dad moves out. When I go to his new house, it's pretty fun. There are toys there and a Super Duper Bike Wash but Dad's is different. Dad says it's better here than Mom's house. Alright! I think Dad's house is better. I love it here and when I went back to Mom's house and she kept asking about how it was at Dad's house, I said the truth. "It's better there". She asked why. I said, "Because it is, there's a Super Duper Bike Wash and everything." Mom said that the water in Dad's Super Duper Bike Wash would make me sick and not to touch it but hers is clean. So when I went back to Dad's house, he asked me why I wasn't playing in my Super Duper Bike Wash. I said, "Because your water is dirty and it will make me sick. I want to go to Mom's and wash my bike."

My dad said Mom doesn't know anything and that's why they are in two different houses. He told me not to listen to Mom because he loves me with all of his heart and wouldn't let anything bad happen to me. He also said that Mom doesn't know anything and his house is better. So I played in the Super Duper Bike Wash and I didn't get sick. Dad was right. When I went back to Mom's house, I was happy to see her. We hugged and she gave me a kiss, it made me feel good. She asked what I did at Dad's house. I said "stuff." She then asked, "You didn't play in the dirty water did you?" I said, "Yes I DID and you don't know anything." I ran to my bedroom. My mom came in right away and said, "Why don't you think I know anything? What did your dad tell you?" I told her, "Dad said not to listen to you because you don't know anything."

My mom looked mad and she told me that Dad doesn't care about me. He just wants me to hate Mommy. "Why?" I asked. She said, "Because what Mommy is doing is right and Dad knows it, so he wants to get you to hate me like he does. You don't have to listen to Dad when you go there, Mommy loves you with all of her heart and would never let anything bad happen to you." I am so confused. I like it at both places. I love both my dad and my mom.

The next time at Dad's, I don't say much; I don't feel like having fun.

The days aren't like they used to be with so much fun to be had and almost no time to do it.

My dad asks, "What's wrong Bud, you don't want to play with your Super Duper Bike Wash?" I just said, "no." I didn't have any fun at Dad's this time. When I got back to Mom's, before she even said hi, she asked what I did and who was there. I am not having any fun at Mom's house either. I could play with the Super Duper Bike Wash but I will get yelled at by one of them. I could watch cartoons but then Mom or Dad just comes in and think I need to talk about something. They ask me if Mom has a boyfriend or if Dad has a girlfriend. They ask and I answer, "I don't know!" I just want to be left alone.

I go to bed and cry as I think; if Mom says she loves me with all of her heart and Dad says he loves me with all of his heart, why do I still feel like crying? I don't think they love me with all of their hearts or they wouldn't have to take love from mine. Since my parents always made me make a choice between vegetables and bedtime, I tried to do the same, give them a choice. I wrote them a note while I was crying silently. I can't write very well yet but it said:

"Luv mee with all of yor heart..............................or leev mee with all of mine".

2. TRAUMA

I wrote this book from my own experiences as a parent over the last thirteen years, and when I was near the end of the book I stumbled upon a name for what I wrote about, as well as a definition. What is happening to the child who wrote the heartfelt letter to his parents is called Hostile Aggressive Parenting; also known as Parent Alienation or PA. This is the process of abusing your child with tactics that turn the child against the other parent. When the alienation is successful, the child will then hate the other parent and everything to do with them, including siblings, grandparents, aunts, and uncles. I will use the definition directly from the Parental Alienation Awareness Organization's website.

Hostile Aggressive Parenting or HAP, is a serious form of child maltreatment and abuse, and is encountered in most high conflict child-custody disputes and often is used as a tool to align the child with one parent during litigation.

The definition I use is as follows:

Parental Alienation: Abuse inflicted on a child by "a parent who hates their ex more than they love their child" (source unknown).

The effects of HAP and PA are awful and range from a child being withdrawn, depressed and angry, to violent, and suicidal.

The first thing I noticed, when I learned the names for these forms of abuse, was the argument over who is the cause of it. Some say fathers are the biggest cause and some say mothers are. Women's groups are fighting with men's groups, professionals against professionals. I thought to myself, how are we as parents supposed to put an end to this if we go from arguing parents, and alienating parents, to parents who can't even stop arguing about whose fault it is? Parental Alienation is gender neutral, both mothers and fathers are guilty of this.

Is there a related condition from which an alienating parent suffers? Perhaps. Was the alienating parent a victim of this abuse by their parents? Possibly. Is there a history of depression and suicide in the family of the alienating parent? Maybe. There are a number of parents who were abused as they were growing up; however, some of these parents are truly wholesome and loving parents, with the drive to give their kids a different life from what they had. So what is the excuse for the remaining parents that have had a hard past, or the ones who have had a great upbringing? If this is a book with the purpose of creating positive change, let's discuss things about which we can't argue.

If we looked at a hundred single child relationships that have become a Hostile Aggressive Parenting situation, maybe seventy-five of the abusing parents are the fathers, and twenty-five are the mothers; or seventy-five of the abusing parents are mothers and twenty-five are fathers. It still equals one hundred abused kids. This isn't about who has custody or primary residence, or who gets the support payments. This isn't about fathers groups or mothers groups. This is about "a parent who hates their ex more than they love their child."

The more people that become aware of these forms of child abuse, the more everyone can start shouting "CHILD ABUSER." If every time we heard parents say things like:

I know you don't want to go to Dad's, but you don't have to listen to him.

Mommy doesn't love you; I'll come get you as soon as I can.

Daddy called but he didn't want to talk to you.

Mommy loves her new boyfriend more than you.

We pointed our fingers and made it known to the alienating parent, to the courts and the authorities, that the parent is guilty of hating their ex more than loving their child. They are abusing their own child and that is disgraceful and should be punishable by law. There could be stickers saying "CHILD ABUSER" that we could stick to their cars and houses, and signs at their work that say "A CHILD ABUSER WORKS HERE," or, we could encourage people to read my book, and stop it from happening in the first place.

I have been alienated for most of my thirteen years as a parent. This form of abuse is not going away but instead is becoming increasingly worse and it is not going to go away unless we are aware of it and make changes to stop it. I believe Parent Alienation can be reduced, stopped, and even fixed. I have lived a life of it, and have suffered through trials and errors; trials and errors can be most painful for the parent, but they are even more so for the child. With a little humour by my side, I have dedicated my life to making positive changes through the worst of times. I have learned from my mistakes, and the most important lesson I have learned is how to spot Parent Alienation immediately, react quickly, and never give up. We can change this anger. One alienating parent, who read only a part of my book, saw what they were doing, made a change, and they couldn't be happier with their life now. After all, if you truly love your child, their happiness will make you happy. So, come along kids, let's start making positive changes.

Where do we start?

We need to learn what abuse and trauma really mean. I believe that part of the problem with alienating parents is that they get so caught up in their

7

tantrums, jealousy, and loss of their control, (which is what controlling people require to make themselves feel better); they can't see that what they are doing is abusing their own child.

There are four different types of child abuse: physical, sexual, emotional, and neglect. I believe they are all worth mentioning because some cases of Parent Alienation have escalated and resulted in child deaths, some with a false accusation of sexual abuse, but mostly what we are talking about is emotional abuse.

Definitions from New World Encyclopedia.com

Child Abuse: Any recent act, or failure to act, on the part of a parent or caretaker, which results in death, serious physical or emotional harm, sexual abuse or exploitation, or an act or failure to act which presents an imminent risk of serious harm.

Emotional Abuse: Failure to provide affection or love; substance abuse or domestic violence in front of the child. The effects often result in various behavioural, emotional, or psychological problems.

Some theories suggest childhood trauma can lead to violent behaviour. Some believe that such violent behaviour can become as extreme as serial murder. I believe that when people think of abuse, or trauma, they associate it with the most awful physical or sexual abuse and ignore the possibility that there can be trauma and abuse without either of those situations. This idea that we can't be abusing our children if we're not hitting them couldn't be further from the truth. Emotional abuse traumatizes a child just as swiftly. It is unforgiving, relentless, and quiet in its path. It slowly destroys children by stripping them of their self-esteem, confidence, emotions, trust, and more. It attacks each child differently. Some may be affected by just one incident, while others are not as severely affected. Children are not as resilient as we think they are. They don't just shake things off their back like a wet dog. An alienating parent, who thinks they have claimed victory, as their child shows hatred to the other parent, is missing one simple fact. Once a child is taught to hate, it will not just be limited to that targeted parent. Although abused children sometimes draw closer to the abuser, they eventually will bite the hand that feeds them because, after all, they have been taught to hate, and that is what they know.

The United Way has a fundraiser called "Success by Six," and its purpose is to help the almost 30% of children out there who aren't ready for school by the age of six. In my opinion, perhaps the increasing number of divorces and separations, especially the increasing number of Hostile Aggressive Parenting and Parental Alienation cases, could be a small, but contributing, factor in why so many children still aren't ready for school at the age of six. If anyone can argue that an alienating parent is mindful enough to educate their child properly, have with their best interests at heart, prepare them for school, and still focus on the destruction of the other parent, then please do email me. I would love to hear your rationale. If anyone can argue that the targeted parent, who is dealing with the stress of fighting for their child's love and is still able to focus fully on the child's best interests without being stressed, email me as well; I would love to hear from both sides as this would be an award winning book: "How To Be An Alienating Parent (Or Alienated Parent) With Zero Stress And Zero Harmful Effects On The Children." It is a lovely thought, but the harsh reality is that both situations are anything but stress free. No matter what we think or say, our children are punished by our stress.

Children forced into a Parent Alienation situation or Hostile Aggressive Parenting atmosphere are suffering from the severe effects of abuse. Everybody, not just parents, must realize this if we're going to push ahead with positive change for our children. If we can start to see the amount of child abuse going on right in front of us, we will be taking a great step forward.

CHILDREN SUFFER
THE WRONGS OF
THEIR PARENTS.

Chief Dan George

3. TRAUMA AND THE ADULT BRAIN

I remember my backyard from when I was about three or so. It was huge and endless fun. There was so much room to run and play. In the yard was an enormous hill. It was so difficult to run up or down. I remember having to use all the power in my body to prevent extreme tumbling. Kicking a ball up the hill was great fun though. I could kick it and it would roll right back down, sometimes too fast to kick it again. Every now and then, I would kick the ball so hard that the ball would roll all the way to the glass patio door. I remember running into that door; not a good feeling.

I returned to our old house twenty years later, and to my shock and dismay, our yard had shrunk considerably. Not because of property changes but because the image formed in my childhood brain was from the perspective of a small child. In reality, the yard was only about twenty-five feet long and maybe fifteen feet wide. The giant hill of my childhood was merely a gradual slope; a ball could barely roll down it fast enough to hit the glass patio door that at one time seemed so far away. My perception of our yard remained the same in my thoughts for many years. I wonder if these perceptions were never corrected, would adults continue to think as children? As you get older and wiser some things will be obvious, such as Santa Claus. However, what about the memories formed as a child and never corrected, like my yard, or hurtful words, yelling and abuse? You will notice that they all have something in common. They all make individuals feel badly about themselves, leading to some sort of trauma. Some may label trauma as Less or More severe on the so-called "Trauma Scale," such as in a child sexual abuse case in Kelowna, British Columbia in the summer of 2010. The judge sentenced the accused man to thirty days with time served as the "tickling" only occurred for ten seconds and was considered to be low on the "Trauma Scale."

I have my own trauma scale and hope one day it will be recognized. It doesn't involve intricate mathematical equations or scientific synopses from formulas that require a beaker to find the results. It is not a complex scale that we need to overthink to try to come up with what must be a complicated answer.

Clint's Trauma Scale

(10 seconds of "tickling") + (30 days of jail time) = A lifetime of emotional hurt and trauma.

Go ahead and test my scale, change it up a bit, let's increase the numbers.

(30 seconds of "tickling") + (90 days of jail time) still = A lifetime of emotional hurt and trauma.

Let's decrease the numbers and see what happens.

(5 seconds of "tickling") + (no jail time) still = A lifetime of emotional hurt and trauma.

If you are still skeptical about my scale, let's try taking sexual abuse out of the equation and adding a different type of abuse (emotional) to the equation.

(One stay at Mom's/Dad's house) + (the parents teaching the child to hate the other parent) = A lifetime of emotional hurt and trauma.

No matter what you put into the equation, the result is always the same.

I believe a child advocate should be appointed in all child cases, separations included. There should be someone to advocate for the child, to understand his or her trauma and potential for negative growth if it should go unseen and untreated. That someone would have experience with children and have an outside point of view, which would focus on the child's best interests and not that of the upset parents and their lawyers. Lawyers are paid for their expertise in separations and dividing things among the divorced for a handsome fee, NOT in child psychology.

To a child, everything is huge, like my yard. Yelling is scary and hurtful and isn't easily forgotten. We can delete things on our computers; however, the information remains inside somewhere. As a computer tech goes into our hard drive and retrieves information that was "deleted", a child professional can also help retrieve information and fix problems with some careful work. Transitions Facilitator, Sue Foisy describes the event of a trauma as:

> Placing the first brick down and starting the foundation. If trauma goes unnoticed, ignored, and untreated, the bricks continue to stack up making this trauma wall bigger and bigger, making it more and more difficult for child professionals to get back to that most important first foundational brick. Depending on how many bricks get placed in this wall there can be new problems arising with new bricks placed on top of the old ones and so on.

> Breaking down this wall to get back to that foundational first brick is a slow and delicate process done with the child's best interests in mind. A child psychologist or counselor must go into the brain of the child with careful intention to find the first underlying brick that started the whole foundation. This emotionally sensitive process is much like peeling back the frail petals of a wilted rose

with the goal of reaching the un-damaged bud at the center and turning it once again into a beautiful flower.

For this reason, it is imperative to see that this type of trauma, although in some cases it may be considered to be less or more severe, be identified and treated from the start, just as any other "serious" trauma would be.

Birds are birds and even though there are many different types or species, one constant remains the same...they are still birds, and trauma is still trauma. The one thing about birds is they mostly flock together, hunt together, eat together, and protect each other and their young.

Some birds do not flock together, or hunt together, or protect each other. These birds are more susceptible to being hunted and, sadly, do not have the support of the flock that would save them.

We, as parents and friends, need to flock together and remember the saying that is oh so true. "It takes a village to raise a child."

It takes a village to raise a child but what we fail to see is when a child is taken from a parent out of anger by the other parent, that child does not just lose their parent. They lose themselves and the entire village.

So where do we go from here?

4. Our Childhood Memories

As I try to remember my earliest times as a child, I don't remember how old I was exactly, but I remember being sick; I saw my mother through a window and having the most uncomfortable feeling in my bottom. When I saw her standing next to me, I felt relief, because I was so scared. She peered over what seemed to be the Hoover Dam, and she handed me a blue stuffed animal. It instantly made me feel safe and quickly became my favorite. Later, I found out it was a 'Smurf,' the uncomfortable feeling in my bottom was a thermometer and the great clear wall was that of the crib in the hospital. "You can't possibly remember that," my mom said, "you were only one!" Well I do, clear as the tall window that she reached over to hand the toy to me.

My next memory I was Kindergarten age. I remember there was fence that divided the two yards. I was five years old and I remember my mom getting me ready for something. I can't remember if it was an appointment or Kindergarten, but I was bathed and in clean new clothes. We had a few extra moments as I was ready early and I asked my mom if I could go outside and play until it was time to go (you know where this is going). By asking, I mean begging over and over again until I saw the vein pop up in Mom's forehead, and I knew I was either on the pathway to success or the bedroom. She was in a hurry and my pleading was indeed rewarded with some outside time before we left, as long as, I did not get dirty! I said what every truthful five year old raring to go outside would say, "I won't," and it won her over. So, outside I went. I don't remember exactly what time of year it was but I assume it was autumn because the backyard, which once was a garden filled with plants, was now a field of dirt. I was a five-year-old boy in a field of dirt, telling Mom I won't get dirty.

I remember trying to be so good; I was not going to get dirty. I would make Mom happy. I tried my best, I really did, but quite honestly, it was painfully boring. The countless minute that went by was tortuous and no longer could I resist the temptation. I picked up a stick and flicked the soil, just a little bit. Well, call it a guy thing, or whatever you want, but as soon as the stick hit the beautiful untouched and unexplored soil and I flicked it into the air, it was like confetti and I just burst the piñata. I was powerless; I dropped to my knees and started digging furiously. I dug frantically, flinging dirt in the air before my time expired. Digging my clean pants, knee-by-knee, deeper into the dirt, I was the painter, the stick was my brush, and the mud was my palate of fun. The garden was now my canvas and I was the master of this thing. Who knew that this could be this much fun! If you take away all the awful things that grow in it that you have to eat, it is actually a lot of fun. So, in the midst of my temporary lack of judgment, I hear my mom call out from the window. "Clint, it's time to go, you're not getting dirty are you?" I looked up at the window and saw the silhouette of my mother. She was watching me, how long was she there? So, I said what every guy would probably say, young or old, when totally busted.... "Nope!" Why did I just say nope? I know I am busted, did I think my mom wouldn't notice the filthy pants? Of course I did. I lied and I actually thought that I would get away with it, (yes ladies, it starts here; now you know), until my mom said calmly "What happened!" and I assure you this is a true story, I replied, "I fell."

I know my mom saw me, digging in the dirt like a dung beetle, and this is my story, "I fell!" Seriously. Well now we're running late and my clothes and I are filthier than when I hit the tub. Expecting the worst, my mom looked at me and smiled, paused, and then said, "C'mon, let's go inside and change." I knew I was in trouble and didn't take the kindness for granted.

Even though I was five years old, I appreciated her letting me off the hook in what was a time of stress for her.

Other stories are popping up in my mind now, one after another. The point of this chapter is that we, as kids, remember the monumental memories and I want to stress the importance of that. As I write this chapter, I find myself remembering more and more childhood stories. Maybe Freud's theories are correct and we do remember everything, but we stuff the memories in the back somewhere and convince ourselves that we've forgotten about them. We may forget the memory itself but we still act as if the memory were vivid.

All the memories we made as kids are in our brains somewhere; maybe we will remember them someday. Perhaps for our protection our brain hides them, I don't know. But I do know that each memory your child is creating now will be there for a lifetime. Make them good ones.

I am not a psychologist but I want you to try the same thing. Go to a quiet place, steep some tea, and start thinking about your earliest childhood memory. See if that sparks more memories that you may have forgotten about. Perhaps it will answer some questions and if not, at least steer you to someone who can.

My parents divorced when I was almost four years old. We lived in, and owned, Pinaus Lake Lodge in Faulkland, BC. I remember the lodge, (our house) and of course the once huge backyard. My sister and I loved playing on the dock where we would catch shrimp in a jar. Then we would go to Dad's barbecue where our favourite treat was the barbecue's leftovers – you know when you use a lot of sauce and what remains on the grill is a hardened charcoaled, but still saucy and kind of chewy in the center, morsel – weird maybe, but we loved it.

I remember my sister sitting on a rocking chair and I thought it would be funny to stack wood under one side. Well the chair tipped and my sister landed on our dad's chainsaw (not running, of course) but that sure ended the fun. She got even with me though because she shoved me over and I landed on one of those spindles onto which businesses used to poke their receipts. Yes, this is despite our house having all the child safety devices available. Anyway, off to the hospital I went.

My point to all of this you ask? Well as you can see, I have an abundance of memories living at Pinaus Lake and I hadn't even reached four years of age. So yes, children aged one, two and three can remember such life events, good and bad, when their adults!

After that, I didn't see my dad much but I can tell you when Mom said he was coming to pick me up; it was the most exciting time in my life – not because life with my step-dad was bad but because you simply cannot replace the love you have for your parents. I didn't care what the truth was or what my mom's perceptions about my dad were, I just wanted to see him.

THERE'S A STORY OF A CHILD WHOSE PARENTS HAD A BABY AND THERE WERE COMPLICATIONS AND THE BABY DIED. WHEN THE CHILD ASKED WHERE HE WAS, THE PARENTS SAID, "WE LOST THE BABY." THE NEXT DAY THE CHILD WAS EXUBERANT IN SAYING, "WHY ARE WE JUST SITTING HERE? WE SHOULD BE LOOKING FOR THE BABY!"

5. Mike's House

My Story of Unseen Emotional Abuse and its Effects

A friend of mine invited me to her older friend's 50th birthday bash at his house. I was assured a good time as there was going to be a barbecue and a poker game later that evening. I arrived at the house and met my friend around back on the patio and she introduced me to Mike, the birthday boy. We began talking, and he soon asked me about my tattoo, a black tribal design from my shoulder down to my wrist which appears unfinished. I showed him its significance as it has the name of one of my sons and the birth sign of the other. It wasn't something he would do but he complimented it anyway.

My friend who had invited me, seemed a little glum but I mingled and talked with a few people who I hadn't seen in a long time. Later my friend started opening up about why she was so down. Her ex-husband was always saying he was going to pick up the kids, but, recently, he hadn't been showing up. Unfortunately, this is not an uncommon event in a separation. As I was giving her some advice about her kids seeing their dad, I had to pause as the birthday boy was always yelling at his kids. If they threw a ball, he yelled that it was wrong, if they threw it too far he yelled that they need to smarten up, if they ran too fast he yelled at them to behave. When he quit yelling long enough to hear our conversation his immediate response was typically old school, the dad should be punished.

"Don't allow him time with the kids, he doesn't deserve it," he said.

Yes, I agreed that the children do not deserve to be excited to see him, waiting with their bags packed, only to be disappointed and sad to discover that he wasn't coming again. This, however, is about the kids and I went on to say that, the kids do deserve time with their dad, but it should be stress free time. We talked about how kids need to be treated with love, and what's best for them. Their needs must come first, not what the ex "deserves." What was she to do though? She was in such a spot. She knew the kids wanted to see their dad, but was worried about hurting them more. I suggested that, before "punishing him" and ultimately punishing the kids, she should talk to him in a very serious but non-threatening way to let him know what he was really doing to them. How much they hurt, how they cry, what they say. The next time he made plans to pick them up, the children wouldn't be told until he knocked on the door and if he continued not showing up, she would have no choice but to change the agreement they had in place.

Of course, between yelling at his kids, Mike had his own input here and there. He actually was trying to give her advice about her children, when in front of everyone he was emotionally abusing his own children. "How can you give her advice when you stand here abusing your own children," I asked. His reply was expected. "I'm not abusing my children, I am disciplining them," he replied.

When discussing views on parenting with Mike, it was obvious that his opinions were very different from mine. Parenting in a "normal family" is very different from single parenting. He argued his point that kids need rules and should know he's in charge or they will take over. Yes, I agreed, kids need rules; however, kids need someone to look up to and respect, not fear. Fear is in our minds and yelling eventually will be called and revealed as nothing more than pathetic. Once the fear is gone, you will have nothing. Respect and being looked up to as a safe provider will last forever. When their fear runs out and they no longer respect you, what do you have? You have a child who has learned not to respect authority, and that child is a danger to himself and everyone around him. As they grow older, they challenge authority; they have no respect, and no sense of consequence. Perhaps this presents itself as not listening to a teacher, maybe its violence. What you're left with is a parent who says they don't know what's wrong with their kids but it all stems from what he was telling me at that very moment! What's wrong with kids today is not that they don't respect authority; it's that they have been stripped of someone to respect, look up to, learn from, and love. I told him my story.

My story:

I grew up in a house filled with yelling. When I found out that yelling was just that, yelling, I felt liberated. I pushed every red button that I shouldn't push. I did it all. At sixteen I was in a drinking and driving accident; at twenty, I overdosed on acid and came close to cardiac arrest.

I hadn't thought about this night in years, yet even now I can rattle off my story like it was yesterday. Trauma remains, even if we don't think about it on a daily basis. I didn't die that night, but came very close. I have not yelled at anyone since then, because of that night. The experience, as it didn't kill me, taught me something. So if you're thinking that yelling isn't traumatic to your kids, think again. Yelling was trauma as I perceived it, and it nearly killed me, and several others.

I started drinking. I drank and drank, when one day, exactly thirty days after I got the license I had painstakingly waited sixteen years for. I was drunk that night. I drank more than half a pub. My friends wanted to go to a party about 30km's away. They all looked to me, as I was the most sober. "Let's roll," I said. We all shared in the stupidity: there were five in the front and six in the truck box of a single cab truck. "I'm fine," I thought as I drove down the windy road that followed the lake just below. My sister was angry, and her boyfriend almost kicked me out of my truck when we stopped at a gas station. Not too far from the party, we were stopped by a police officer. He talked to me while everyone in the back ducked down, and he didn't notice. I asked him for directions, and he pointed out the way. I couldn't stop now. I was in the clear; the cop just waved me through. I was untouchable. When we got to the party, there was no place to park and I heard people talking about my sister's boyfriend looking for me. I panicked. Imagine, I had no respect for authority, but I was afraid of my sister (who I loved and respected) and her boyfriend. I turned around and started back down the long, dark road. Either the people in the cab of my truck, or the loud music must have distracted me. I can't be sure; I don't remember the stop sign, or them yelling for me to stop. I just kept driving at 130 km an hour.

An oncoming car at the intersection, which had right of way, struck us. I wasn't sure what happened; I didn't feel anything. I just looked out my window and we came to a stop in an orchard, down a slight culvert. The truck was on all four tires but leaning, I heard screams, people ran. What have I done? I thought. There was no one in my truck box. I looked around. No bodies. My heart was pounding so hard I'm sure it was showing on the outside. I heard someone yell, "Get out of here." I turned around I saw a car turned sideways in the intersection, hood crinkled, steam, or what appeared to be steam, billowing out from under the hood. I slowly approached the car to see if they were alive. It was an elderly couple. The woman was lying motionless in the passenger seat and her husband, started screaming, "She's dead!"

In the background, I heard sirens faintly growing louder with every pounding heartbeat. The ambulance came, police cars everywhere. Me, crying on the ground, concerned about the lady in the passenger seat. Then it hit me. My truck was also in the opposite direction from where I was headed, and as my eyes followed the lights from the police searching the orchard, for the first time I wondered if that's why I hadn't seen anyone. Are they all dead in the orchard? Still breathing, I thought, what have I done?

I was handcuffed and put in the back of the police car. I was taken downtown and probably blew over the equivalent of an entire pub. Thank the Lord no one was seriously hurt. The lady in the passenger seat was knocked out, but recovered and my friends, who were in my truck box, were also fine. They had all ran through the orchard, afraid that they would get into trouble for riding in the truck box.

I lost my license for a year, and was put on probation for a year-and-a-half. I also had to attend alcohol counseling, which, to me at the time, was a joke. A bunch of messed up kids dumber than a turtle, listening to a counselor tell them things would be ok, and that they should share their feelings. These kids needed much more than counseling; they needed a ride in my truck box. I got along with the counselor though; he was nice. He understood that I wasn't a raging teen alcoholic. What I didn't know at the time was what he was really doing – he was getting at my anger issues and my lack of respect for authority.

When court was all said and done, I was sued by ICBC for $17,000, which my stepdad settled for $5,000. I was forced to quit drinking. The counselors didn't like it much because I couldn't be in alcohol counseling if I didn't drink, and they hadn't cracked my authority and anger issues yet. So I thought to myself, well, I've done the worst and everything is ok. Yell away. What's left? Well, drugs, of course.

What's more frightening than any horror show out there? A teenager who no longer appreciates, respects, or fears authority; I mean really, what were they going to do to me? I had done the worst, drank, crashed my truck, and I didn't care much at the time. What were they going to do? Yell at me? I didn't kill the old lady and my friends were fine. Authority what? Authority who? Put me in a school class where I don't have to do as much and get praised for what most school kids get D's for? Great.

So I started doing drugs. I started with marijuana. It made me dizzy and weird. I didn't like it all that much until one night, when I'd had a few beers, and I smoked a little hit. Wow. I had found my true love. I didn't have to buy many beers, and five bucks worth of weed would last forever. Until that forever came and my boredom got the best of me. After that, it was gloves off. Let's do it. Before I knew it, I was sniffing everything I could put on a mirror, and sticking every hallucinogen under my tongue...or munching it. When you're that high, beer no longer has an effect on you. You could drink a thousand beers, but it was more of a social have-something-in-your-hand, kind of drinking.

One evening, a friend had picked up some acid that was "double dipped." That meant instead of just a dropper of the drug on the paper, it was dipped right in, dried, and then dipped again. I decided to take two, which was the equivalent of sixteen hits of acid.

We met some friends, and one of them invited us over to her house for a while, as her parents were out for the evening. She warned us to get out, and do it quickly when they came home. Her dad was a drunk, and a mean one. He would beat the family just for something to do. Weighing in at about 350lbs, he spent most of his time with his logger buddies, drinking and picking up trees, I'm sure, on his own. Everyone was afraid of him. Everyone except me; what is he going to do, yell at me? I laughed.

As the evening went on, I got higher and higher. We were jumping on the trampoline with the sprinklers on below. Every time I jumped, it felt like I was riding a wave, up and down. The feeling was intense. I was having so much fun when my friend came running and shouted, "They're here, they're here, and you gotta go." Me? Go? "Who does he think he is," I thought in my obviously not-so-clear mind. They pulled up into the carport as my friend was begging me to leave. Now I'm not too sure if it was my own arrogance or my friend's obvious fear, but I wasn't leaving. I found myself yelling at him on the hood of his car when he pulled in. I'm not sure what I was yelling; I was just yelling and cursing him.

The carport dropped off about a foot or two at the side, to the crushed gravel driveway below where his camper was stored. I was at the side of the car by the time he opened his door, and it hit me. I lost my balance and fell off the unexpected drop to the gravel driveway below, tripping and stumbling until I finally stopped. I hit the camper and it broke my fall. I braced my arms to take the impact. My left arm was ok, while my right arm managed to brace itself through the camper window. I panicked, it happened so fast but I guess pulling my arm back out did the most damage. Blood instantly started to pool on the ground. What's worse, my friend's drunken Dad came after me, thinking I had smashed out his camper window on purpose. I ran for my life.

I ran to the nearby grocery store where a janitor was standing at the back of his van. I begged him to save me. He was scared, obviously. A kid running up to him, covered in blood that was spraying everywhere, with a mean-looking fellah chasing him. I tried grabbing a mop bucket, anything I could, but it was no use. I had lost too much blood and was getting weak. I fell to my knees, only to be picked up by my hair and dragged back across the street. He said he was calling the cops; I begged him to do so. "I'm dying," I said, choking on blood and vomit as he continued to beat me. I wilted and fell to the ground.

When I came to, I saw red and blue lights. You would think this was my saviour, what I was waiting for. Unfortunately, in my mind, it was another authority figure. I started yelling at them. It took them some time to cuff me and throw me in the car, kicking and yelling. Blood was all over the back of the police car. I was yelling, I don't remember what, but I heard the police officers saying, "What is Yahee?" According to the police report, I was yelling about how I wished my life was the way it was before, no yelling, just fun, and playing board games with my family, the way it used to be.

When we got to the hospital, the two kind officers escorted me into the emergency room, my pants down to my knees, me telling everyone to...well, you get the picture. My pants, shirt, and face were covered in blood, and I was still leaving a trail of blood on the floor as they carried me in.

25

These were people who were going to help me, but I was too far-gone. I yelled at the people in the waiting room, I yelled at the doctors in the emergency room. I yelled until they pushed me face down on a hospital bed, and restrained my hands and feet. As I turned my head, which was all I could move, I could just barely see the door. The nurse gave me the finger.

I woke up a day-and-a-half later at home, the ring on my right hand encrusted with dried blood. I wasn't sure if it was an actual wound, or from the blood that had been dripping from my arm. Turned out it was just too caked in blood to slip it off.

The hockey playoffs were on, so my mom turned on the game for me. I watched only a few minutes before my body started cramping up, first the fingers, then hands. My hands pulled tightly toward each other and then across my arms, my arms closer to my chest, and my legs following up to my abdomen. I yelled for my mom. She ran in and told me that they said this would happen. "What would happen?" I yelled. "Withdrawal, we need to get you back to the hospital," she told me. I could barely walk, and she almost carried me to the car. When we arrived at the hospital, I couldn't budge. I was a crumpled up mess. Two hospital staff helped me inside and sat me down in an emergency room chair. I kept sliding off, and my mom kept lifting me back up.

Finally, they carried me into the emergency room where the doctor gave me a needle. Instantly my body relaxed; what a feeling. The doctor looked at me and said, "Mr. Williams, I am not here to harp or play your parents' roll, but two nights ago you almost went into cardiac arrest. Your family was here and we thought you would die that night. Your family loves you very much and I would like you to look seriously into drug rehab, as well as counseling for anger management. You got lucky Mr. Williams, I don't know why, but I suggest you use this as your second, or last, chance." Since that day, I have not touched a single drug.

Two years later, my first son was born. I had a tattoo done around my bicep with my sons' name on it. The tattoo however, did nothing to cover the scar down my arm from that night and was a constant reminder. Every time I worked out and lifted the weight to the top, there it was. Every time I lifted a fork to my mouth, I saw it in the corner of my eye, a horrific night playing over and over, year after year, in my mind. I decided to cover up the scar with another tattoo to help forget the pain. I started from the shoulder down, leaving the inside of my arm for last, as it was the least seen by others. I planned eventually to work my way to covering up the huge scar, with the hope of not being constantly reminded of not only the night I nearly died, but also of all my nights, the yelling, who I had become. I ran out of money and while trying to save up to finish covering the scar, something changed inside me. I began instead, to see my arm as a motivational piece and decided not to cover the scar. The inside of my arm is scarred; a memory of what happened to me when the negativity and trauma got the better of me; when the rebellion, the yelling, and lack of respect ruled my life. The outside of my arm has a tattoo of my elder son's name and my younger son's birth sign, the two most important people in my world. Some may look at my tattooed outer arm and question my ethics. To me, it reflects my saving grace. While my inner arm, no longer a memory of horror is a positive reminder of who I will never be again nor have my children become. Johnny Cash wore black for the unfortunate and ill-treated and I wear this black on my arm for the children who have the same fate. You won't see any colors on my arm until maybe, I too, can ease a little of the darkness off my back.

I told this story at the party I mentioned earlier. After I finished my story, I turned to Mike and said "Now let's go back a bit friend, and you tell me, if yelling isn't child abuse and trauma. When this happens to your kids, and it will, what are you going to do? Lock them up? Beat them? For one, you'll go to jail, and two, it will make your kids worse. You'll be thinking to yourself, I don't know where I went wrong, completely missing the fact that abuse comes in different forms, and isn't just about what you see on the outside.

He looked at me with glassy eyes and said, "Well what do you think I should do?" Wow, what a tough question for me to answer. I'm not a counselor or psychologist, so I gave him the same advice I'm giving you now, via this book. I can tell you how I stopped it and what I have learned over the past thirteen years of trial and error. I can tell you about everything I've learned from the works of great psychologists like Dr. Gordon Neufeld and Dr. Warshak, but I am not a master of parenting. I recommend you read Dr. Gordon Neufeld's books, or take his courses as I did to understand how to reach out and understand your children, have them look up to you. They should look up to you, not out of fear, but out of respect, love, and loyalty.

I told Mike to consider his kids as his poker hand. As Johnny Cash once said, "You gotta know when to hold 'em, know when to fold 'em, know when to walk away, know when to run." "Right now, I said, "you have a full house, not a bad hand to have. Don't gamble on that. I suggest to you, that you take your full house and you hold 'em."

I later heard that after I walked away, he was crying. That night he tucked his kids into bed, and passed on the poker game.

As parents, we are given a false sense of assurance that simply because we are now parents, we naturally know everything about parenting. What we don't know will simply just arrive as an automatic parenting instinct, protecting our children from harm's way and raising them to be the best they can be. Parents are well educated and equipped with books on the process of pregnancy and what to expect in the delivery room. Then there is usually a nurse that checks on the parents shortly after, weighs the baby, makes sure all is well and that the parents are taking care of their baby.

What about the books and education after that? Sure we can teach our children to be safe, not to run with scissors or run across the road; but what about truly understanding our children? How do we understand where our children are emotionally coming from and what they need from us as parents? How do parents learn about the damage being done to the child if parents don't understand or just shrug off the warning signs as a bad kid in need of disciplining?

It is assumed that parents will just know how to parent, but it is acceptable to admit that we need more education to be the best parents we can be, for our children and ourselves. Educating yourself as a parent and truly understanding YOUR children is a step in the right direction. I encourage you to do as I did and look up the works of Dr. Gordon Neufeld. His book "Hold On To Your Kids," has changed my life and the lives of my boys.

6. WE ARE BREEDING OUR CHILDREN TO HATE

I say breed and I say hate because this isn't parenting. Parenting is creating a child out of love, raising them out of love, and teaching them and watching them grow out of love. Parent Alienation is nothing like this; it is simply breeding a new species of children, ones that hate and don't respect others. Ones that are depressed, violent or suicidal. This is not parenting. What it is, is nauseating and it's abuse.

If you tie a string on the right-hand side of a young plant, that's the way it will grow. If you tie the string to the left that's the direction it will grow. We teach our kids to hate until they are old enough to make their own decisions, then ignore any responsibility, expecting them to do well, and then frown upon their mistakes. Why don't we raise our kids to love, and then let them make their own choices as adults?

The one thing a child needs most is a wholesome loving environment. If that means one environment or two, it is still a must for your child's future. If you have your child on weekends only, then provide that wholesome loving environment all weekend, not hatred. They will remember their time with you, even if it is two days a week. Those two days a week could be shaping your child more than you know.

If we just put our hate aside and let the kids go to their mom's or dad's, without either parent trying to win the battle and instead simply providing the best, wholesome loving environment for them, what a good place our children will be in. They don't have to know that you haven't let your anger toward your former spouse go, they will just know that they are happy with you. When they are older and see the truth, they will make their own judgments. Until then, wouldn't it be nice to know that even if you (both of you) had to bite your tongue, it would create a loving child? Trust me, even though it seems like the most difficult thing to do, you will thank yourself for what you did for your child.

7. RATIONAL ALIENATION VERSUS IRRATIONAL ALIENATION

While I was writing this book, I was asked for advice by people dealing with separation woes. One of the things I would say is that it is ok to tell your child if the other parent is unsafe to be around. After reading Dr. Warshak's book, "Divorce Poison," I learned that I was on the right track. There are names for this kind of thing. Rational Alienation is when a child is made aware of the parent's actions, not out of hatred, but for his or her own safety. Irrational Alienation is when a child is taught or made to hate the other parent because of personal issues, such as jealousy. Here is a list of things to look for if you suspect Parent Alienation and it comes directly from Dr. Richard A. Warshak's book, "Divorce Poison."

Is Your Child Irrationally Alienated?

Professionals disagree on how to label children who reject a parent for no good reason, but they agree on the characteristics of children suffering from this disturbance. If children have several of these signs, consider having them evaluated for pathological alienation.

Unreasonable, persistent, negative attitudes (anger, hatred, fear, distrust, or anxiety) about a parent who was viewed more favorably in the past. Such attitudes often are freely expressed to the parent and others.

No apparent guilt for treating the parent with malice, contempt, and utter disrespect; exploits parent by accepting money and gifts without gratitude.

Explanations for the hatred or fear that are trivial, irrational, inadequate, and out of proportion to the rejected parent's behavior (or false allegations of abuse).

One-sided views of parents: children describe the alienated parent exclusively or predominantly in negative terms and deny or minimize positive feelings, thoughts, or memories about that parent. By contrast, children describe the other parents as nearly perfect.

In any conflict between the parents, the children automatically support the favored parent without exercising critical thinking or considering other perspectives. Some children ask to testify against a parent in court.

Parroting adult language: The children's expressions echo the alienating parent – often clearly beyond the child's normal vocabulary and understanding – or concern adult matters such as court motions, evidence, and testimony.

Preoccupation with the favoured parent while in the rejected parent's presence, including frequent and lengthy phone conversations and texting.

Declaration of Independence: The children profess that their rejection of one parent is their own decision and that the other parent had no influence on the alienation.

Hatred by association: The children denigrate and reject relatives, friends, even pets associated with the rejected parent, despite a previous history of gratifying relations."

8. THE STRESS OF BEING THE ALIENAT"ING" PARENT VERSUS THE STRESS OF BEING THE ALIENAT"ED" PARENT

When I first learned about Parent Alienation, I was shocked to discover that the arguments surrounding it were focused on who was the cause, rather than the solution. There are a lot more factors to consider than simply whose fault it is. Things like: Is it a mental issue? Is it a controlling issue? It's time to stop the excuses and start examining the real causes.

Let's not label it a mental thing, let's just label it a pathetic condition of someone who is angry and wants revenge for their own self-fulfillment, even if it means abusing their children. The problem is that Parent Alienation is becoming a common thread among angry and jealous parents.

Alienat"ing" parents continues to punish themselves in their fight for victory. How many people do you know who are battling a bitter divorce that are truly happy? The alienat"ed" parent has his or her own set of stresses; dealing with this set of stresses in everyday life as an alienat"ed" parent means they are not able to concentrate on their lives, work or relationships. Even though the alienat"ed" parent is experiencing a very difficult and trying time as they try to save both their child's and their own sanity, they manage. They are the parents who are stronger, they are the parents who trudge through the day with a smile because that is what's best for their children and while some might not have a lot of money, they all fall into the same category. They are parents who are, or will be truly happy themselves, and happy for their children. They have the respect of their friends, their family, and their children.

The alienat"ing" parent usually continues to dig his or her own hole deeper and deeper. Stress piles up and when it seems that they have won the hate war, they, like most wars, have won nothing at all. People are tired of hearing them complain without a thought of changing or bettering themselves. Eventually their support system fades; it's simply a matter of time. If they succeed, as the years go by, they will find themselves explaining to their child, who they now want in their lives, about what they went through, and how they are sorry. By this time a simple sorry won't cut it. Once you teach a child to hate, that child will eventually bite the hand that feeds them because that is what they know, hate. The parent who stuck it out, sucked it up and truly did what was best for their child will be the victor. Not only will they be the victors for their children, but also for their children's children as the victory won't be over the ex but over emotional abuse.

Whatever side you are on; when there is an alienat"ing" parent involved it is stressful for both parents. In both cases the child loses, either by the alienat"ed" parent becoming an alienat"ing" parent, as a result of trying to combat the attack and saying things that shouldn't be said; or by the alienat"ing" parent focusing all their energy on their goals and forgetting, not only about their kids, but also their own well-being.

Try this equation in Clint's Trauma Scale:

(1 stressed out parent) + (1 stressed out parent) + (a child/children)
= A lifetime of emotional trauma and hurt.

It is imperative for parents to understand that in this fit of jealousy and power struggle, they are destroying their kids. I believe these parents love their children greatly, but they are blinded by their anger or jealousy. If the same love that makes them abuse their children unknowingly can be reflected to show them the truth, that love, when applied to the good, will be as it should be - uncorrupted.

9. Things to Do During and After a Break-up

So you've finally made the big step. The break-up day has arrived. You think it is going to be the start of a new beginning. Well, before you start to think everything is going to be cloud hopping, understand that if you have a child together, or if one is on the way, there will be no cloud nine for you to jump on. Depending on how you and your ex act, it can be good or it can be the start of bad things to come....

Here's a little exercise I do which can help with everyday things not just with your kids:

Close your eyes; what you see is darkness, with the exception of the last light you saw that flickers like a strange colour. Eventually it fades.

Picture yourself on the left, now your ex on the far right, now your child or children in the middle. Now slowly blur yourself out so you can only see your silhouette but not yourself. Skip over to the right and blur your ex to the same blurred silhouette. What do you see clearly? Your children. You may dislike your ex, but when you blur that out, you see what really matters. Your children.

Whatever the source of your anger toward them, it is nothing in comparison to what really matters. The only clear thing is your kids. Both of you should put your

hatred to rest and work as a team to protect what is clear.
You have plenty of time down the road to waste your
own time with hatred and jealousy, but not until your
kids are fine and on their own.

I will say that ignoring problems isn't the best way to get over them but sometimes, when there are other situations that need immediate attention, something that has no end in sight needs to be overlooked. Understand that you, yourself personally, have the right to think that now you can move on with your life, but you don't have the right to forget everyone involved and only look forward to a life of doing whatever you want. There are two of you and, most importantly, at least one child. The day of your break-up is the first day of forgetting about you, your stress, your anger and jealousy. It is about starting to think about what's in the best interests of your child. Your life is going to change drastically, so accept it. You will have to move on in life but do not think this happens instantly. This will be a process of time and change done with your children's best interests in mind. You have to try, as parents, to come up with a situation that is best for your child. If you don't, a judge who doesn't know either of you, the ex, or the child, will make that decision for you.

It is time to quit making excuses and pointing the finger saying, "Shame on you." Hopefully, if we can admit to what the problem really is, we can then learn how to fix it. Understand that, in one way or another you chose to have this child with that person.

A life of being single can be great; you make your own choices, decisions on where you want to go, want to eat, etc. When you get involved in a relationship, things change. You now find yourself having to be flexible with those things. Many of us these days get caught up in "love at first sight," and forget about protection and end up pregnant. Before you get pregnant, both people must be sure that they want a life-long relationship with the other. If you thought you had to be flexible in a regular relationship, once a child is brought into the relationship it is no longer about you, it's about the child. There are two parents and both have a right to the child (with exceptions of course).

Understand that there is a process we go through when we encounter loss called the "Kübler-Ross Model," also known as The Five Stages of Grief. This model was created by Dr. Elisabeth Kübler-Ross, M.D. and was introduced in her book, "On Death and Dying." The five stages are a process people go through when they have experienced a loss in their life. This could be a loss associated with their own upcoming death, but has also been recognized as the stages seen in most types of loss such as: a death of a loved one, the loss of a relationship or job, drug addiction and many other types of loss. The individual doesn't have to be the love-smitten one either. Spending time with someone in a relationship creates attachment.

There is no time limit on how long an individual takes to get through these stages and it is not always the case that they will experience all of them or even in order. Everyone is different and is affected by a loss or trauma differently. What is important is that you recognize this as a normal process and understand it. You are not alone and you are not weird or crazy. It is important for the individual to have a great support system of family and friends who understand this process and continue to support you until you have reached the acceptance stage.

These are Dr. Elisabeth Kübler Ross's Five Stages of Grief:

Denial—"I feel fine."; "This can't be happening, not to me."

Denial is usually only a temporary defense for the individual. This feeling generally is replaced with a heightened awareness of positions and individuals that will be left behind after death.

Anger—"Why me? It's not fair!"; "How can this happen to me?"; "Who is to blame?"

Once in the second stage, the individual recognizes that denial cannot continue. Because of anger, the person is very difficult to care for because of misplaced feelings of rage and envy. Any individual who symbolizes life or energy is subject to projected resentment and jealousy.

Bargaining—"Just let me live to see my children graduate."; "I'll do anything for a few more years."; "I will give my life savings if...."

The third stage involves the hope that the individual can somehow postpone or delay death. Usually, the negotiation for an extended life is made with a higher power in exchange for a reformed lifestyle. Psychologically, the individual is saying, "I understand I will die, but if I could just have more time..."

Depression—"I'm so sad, why bother with anything?"; "I'm going to die... What's the point?"; "I miss my loved one, why go on?"

During the fourth stage, the dying person begins to understand the certainty of death. Because of this, the individual may become silent, refuse visitors, and spend much of the time crying and grieving. This process allows the dying person to disconnect from things of love and affection. It is not recommended to attempt to cheer up an individual who is in this stage. It is an important time for grieving that must be processed.

Acceptance—"It's going to be okay."; "I can't fight it, I may as well prepare for it."

In this last stage, the individual begins to come to terms with his mortality or that of his loved one.

It is easy to be in one of these stages and not see our actions, but we should try to be mindful of our children throughout this process. When the acceptance stage is reached and you can reflect on the past, will you see a happy child, or a child who is now lost?

Whether the loss is a key person, a desired position or a powerful illusion, each deserves the respect of mourning. The pit in the stomach, the clenched fists and quivering jaw, the anguished sobs prove catalytic in time. In mystical fashion, like spring upon winter, the seeds of dissolution bear fruitful renewal. – Mark Gorkin "The Stress Doc"

Things to do:

Both of you need to put aside your anger and jealousy and breathe in and out slowly. Think about the future of your children before you start fighting about who gets the big screen.

Take a "parenting after separation" course. It will help direct your focus toward your children and it is often mandatory for court, should you take that route. Don't stop there. Take additional courses; they don't take much time and they will benefit everyone, most importantly your child. If you're anything like many parents, myself included, you may think you know enough about your kids and that these silly courses are a waste of time. They seem so obvious and pointless. I assure they are not. I encourage you to take some parenting courses and apply some of the techniques learned. Trust me on this; they will make a remarkable positive difference. Dr. Gordon Neufeld's book, "Hold On To Your Kids" and his online videos helped me truly understand my children and my parenting relationship with them. It is imperative that you get outside of your angry mind, see the other sides of your situation, and understand that you are not alone.

Contact a lawyer, even if you don't end up using one. What I discovered was that having a lawyer who knows you and the situation from the very beginning is a good idea. Usually you can get a free first consultation. If you and your ex start finding things are getting bad and the fighting is getting worse as your ex begins to transmogrify into an alienating parent, you do not want to be left scrambling. I have found that having a relationship with your lawyer from the very beginning is beneficial because if you honestly are doing what is best for your child, they will know. A talk with a lawyer at the beginning will not only give you a realistic impression of how things are, and what the possible outcomes could be, but they will also give you peace of mind knowing that at least someone is on your side. Keep in mind they have seen and heard it all. Always be honest with your lawyer, as lawyers, without a doubt, are better soldiers to have on your

BargainBookStores.com

4860 Danvers Drive SE
Grand Rapids, MI 49512

Order #: 715452
Name: [illegible]
Seller Order: [illegible]
Ship Method: Standard
Order Date: [illegible]
Email: [illegible]
[illegible]

715452

QTY	LOC	Item ISBN	Condition	Price
1	C11	0987785001 Love Me With All of	New	$16.46

Thank you for your order!

Questions: bn@bargainbookstores.com

Subtotal		$16.46
Shipping		$3.99
Total		$20.45

Returns: http://bargainbookstores.com/content/BN_Returns.htm

side rather than against you. The courts want to see what is best for the children not what is best for just you.

Keep doing things that are in your child's best interests. Learn from the courses you take and no matter what, stick to them! Your ex might frustrate you no end. Trust me, they will not just vanish or stay out of your life forever. The ultimate victory, however, will be the happiness of your child, and it will be thanks to you.

Keep a daily journal. Have a record from as soon as the break-up commences. You will need to combat the lies later and a journal is a great way to do that. (You will read more about the court process in the next chatper).It is useful to be able to show any patterns that the child has been used to, and for how long. If your ex says you were never around, but you were, your journal means that you have a fighting chance. If they say they were around and weren't, again you have that documented in your journal.

Do not lie, eventually you will be caught; one lie gets mixed up with another and will almost always be disproved eventually. If you get caught in a lie, most of the good you have done just becomes discredited.

Keep in mind that just because your ex doesn't love you, this doesn't mean they do not love their children with all of their heart and the same goes for you.

If your child no longer has contact with the other parent, and you still think that your child is doing great and that they have everything – guess again – they don't! No matter how much money you throw at them, they will eventually seek what is more important. They will ask about their mother or father and, assuming the other parent is the one who left and never kept in contact, you should tell them the truth and be honest. Know that being honest is what's best for your kids. If you are open and honest, they will love and respect you for doing everything you could rather than despise you for keeping them from the truth.

Parents, no matter how much they hate each other, need to be on the same page. The child does not benefit from parents trying to outdo each other. If one parent lets the child stay up late to gain favouritism, it will backfire. If one parent lets the child eat junk food when they should be eating their supper, it will affect the child's nutrition and get them in trouble with the other parent.

There are two types of parents, ones who are still with their partners and ones who are not. If you fall into the "are not" category, welcome, and this book is a step in the right direction. Things can be better, things can be great, but it starts with the all-important first step.

Usually the ones "doing the most wrong" are the ones who think they are the "most right." This helps their mind justify their poor choices, negative feelings and actions. This makes it difficult to get through to them. If your ex refuses to take a parenting course, say something like, "You may not need these courses but I think I could benefit from them and want us to be on the same page. Could you come with me, or can I give you the dates so you can go on your own?" If they won't, take the course anyway, then do what you can to make life better for your child. You can feel good knowing that you are doing what is best for your child.

IF I DON'T FIGHT WITH
MY BROTHER ANYMORE,
WILL YOU COME BACK
AND LIVE WITH US?

12 year old boy

10. Courts, Legal Fees And The Process

Excerpt from my Journal:

November 17, '09

I was supposed to pick up my son last weekend but was denied access. This weekend again, I was denied access with yet another excuse. I am trying to keep positive but can't help but feel stressed for both of us. The excuses keep piling up and, of course, eventually even implied sexual abuse, which took things to a whole new level of stress (an alienating parent may accuse the ex with sexual abuse usually when their other plans are failing). Her lawyer talked to my lawyer for an hour. $$$$$! I had a hard time keeping my cool because of the lies my ex is telling. It seems that people can make up whatever they want because in court it is a simple "he said, she said." I am thinking that this honest way is not paying off. I talked to a friend today who assured me that I am doing the right thing. So far, it has cost me an extra $760 a month in new vehicle costs, fuel, long distance charges and insurance increases, and still she denies me access, and then applies for monthly maintenance fees. So, as a single dad of a thirteen-year-old in hockey, my bills have increased by $760 a month, plus the thousands in

45

lawyer's fees, roughly $1060 per month as I pay my sister back for my lawyer's fees, and the $300 a month that she puts on her credit card. I have been doing this for over a year now. My three-year-old hates me, his brother, and even the family dog. There are another few months of this just to find out if we can agree before court. I am exhausted and, at this point, if anyone can say they are doing things with a clear head and making appropriate choices for their children with no stress to the children, they are simply lying or worse – they honestly believe that!

No matter what has happened, unless it's about abuse, in court you are in front of a judge who has heard it all and isn't interested in looking at the pointless fighting and lies. My lawyer said, "The problem is that she is saying this and you are saying that and no matter who is honest and who is lying out of anger, the court hears both sides." You can spend years of your life doing what's right, only to get to court and hear, "Well she says this." It's an unfair game, but one that is played every day.

My advice is to document everything after a break-up, from phone calls to pick-ups and drop-offs, have some sort of proof. Even if you have been paying for everything, gas, daycare, etcetera, all that has to happen is for the other parent to say, "No, I have been paying." And unless the lawyers and judge have proof, they will take that as the truth. Really, how do you make a decision as a lawyer or judge when you don't have the evidence? You just hear the bickering like a principal hears schoolyard excuses. It doesn't matter what happened on the school field at lunch, you are both paying for it even if you were the one who got punched.

If you have not yet had the pleasure of riding the lovely trail of The Court Process, saddle up and come along, but first, you will need a few things. Grab your helmet to prevent any shock to your cranium, your big black boots to trudge through the eternal pasture of mud, and your tight pants with one pocket (you won't need any more pockets, the lawyers will have taken care of them). Now you are ready to saddle up your steed, (you will probably have to sell your vehicle anyway), and join me on this most enjoyable ride – The Court Process.

First of all, you will make the initial appointment with a lawyer – hopefully this one is free. Your lawyer will give you all the various routes you can take; you won't like many of them. You have to remember that you are still thinking from a place of hate; as lawyers, they are thinking rationally about the situation and your children. You will refuse; possibly thinking there is still no way that you will settle for that. At this stage, you might seek other legal advice and when they tell you the same thing, you will pout, and then think about it, then settle for the least expensive options available.

You will have to attend a Parenting After Separation course where you will learn that what you are doing is wrong. Hopefully, this helps you understand what your child is going through.

Then you will have to go to mediation. Remember, the courts don't want to decide your child's fate. They give parents every chance to negotiate beforehand. Keep in mind that your bill goes up every time you call your lawyer and every time they get a fax. Every time they talk to the other lawyer, it goes up. Let's say at a modest rate of $275 per hour, this adds up rather quickly so you may not want to rant on the phone with them for too long, or too often. I will tell you that I took the lawyer route and all too soon discovered that my bill was already over $4000.

Now the mediation process is very important. You may go into this still stubborn and disagreeable thinking that you are not going to bend, and take your chances on the judge making the final say. If you take this route, what you will likely find out is that you still didn't get what you wanted, you are thousands in debt and should have negotiated in mediation. Remember, the judges have seen every kind of case over and over again. They know what is and what is not reality. They have to make a decision based on what they feel is best for the child. All of your lies will be called out and you will look foolish. Unless, of course, it is a viable concern, in which case every parent suspecting potential harm to his or her child should be concerned. At the moment, I am talking more about fabricated situations.

If you take the mediation route, it is still a legal document and you have the chance to see how it goes, and it's free! If you decide against mediation, or one of you has, you need a good reason for it. Then, and only then, will they give you a paper that permits you to go to court. This paper you will give to your lawyer and she/he will get things going at a small rate of a couple of hundred dollars per hour, give or take. Now I don't know what you make, but you may see where my problem comes in. I make $21 per hour and pay my lawyer $275 per hour. It's like investing in something that costs me $275 per hour and in return my profits will be $21 per hour. Take that idea to CBC's tv show, Dragons' Den and see how far it goes.

Now the fun part begins – the lawyers start talking. Sometimes, you have two lawyers who are on the same page, or you might not. So one lawyer suggests a change, and the other lawyer says no to that change because their client said so. Their continuous tantrum makes it impossible to make things work, and because of the tantrum-induced refusals, things go nowhere except financially up.

To make it even better, this is the time when the lies start coming out. Whew! Grab the reins and hold on, things which are absolutely ridiculous start appearing. Your ex will say whatever they can to make you look bad and unfortunately your lawyer has a tough time with this because it's the classic 'he said/she said' story. If they say you sniff horse testicles every second Sunday, you have to prove you don't. So you find yourself starting to play the same game to combat their lies. You both think that you are beating the other, that is, until court time where the judge will call you both out on your childish shenanigans and tell you to grow up and do what's best for your child.

Your first court appearance will arrive; this is simply to review the past and current situation and for the judge to order that things remain the same until the next scheduled case conference. This will be another few months away. In the meantime, you will likely continue what you are doing – fighting and hating each other more by the day. This is where my own situation turned around.

Our lawyers fought desperately to agree on something, even if it was something little, so we were at least agreeing on something and not wasting the court's extremely expensive time. We did. It wasn't great, but we did agree and it was a little better. We agreed to try a temporary agreement until our first case conference, and then we could reassess the situation. Before the case conference, our lawyers got together and tried to agree with us again. This time around, it worked a little better and the courts were forgiving because we were working together and they allowed us to review again, without the judge making the ultimate decision.

If this doesn't happen, you will end up with the judge making the final decision. You will have no say and that will be that! The downside, again, is that your expensive lawyer bills get considerably worse every time you step inside the courthouse. The upside is that progress is starting to take place but remember this all could have been done by mediation. So now you are either upset because you think you lost or happy because you think you have won. Most of the time, neither of you get what you want but become ok with the change at the mere cost of your legal fees.

Things you were adamant about refusing, won't seem so bad in court. These lesser agreements now sound appealing rather than the risk of losing. So you end up agreeing on something you could have achieved through mediation.

The following notes show the frustrations that occurred in my case:

Spent $275 per hour for initial consultation, after the free one.

More time for my lawyer to think of the route we should go equals more money owed.

Paid for every letter, email, fax and telephone call.

Paid for her to write out the application and paid for her secretary to type it. Just hope she is a fast typist!

Paid for the first court appearance.

Paid for the follow-up afterward, before the second court date.

Paid to be in court for the second time.

After all of this, we finally agreed on something! As a result, the judge didn't have the final say, and my bill stopped constantly growing.

My total bill equaled $6,750 even after I avoided the final round of court appearances. If you go through the entire process, your fees will likely be double that number when it is all said and done. Imagine the difference in my son's quality of life if my ex and I hadn't fought at all, and I had $6,750 to put toward his best interests. He could have had a great start toward his college tuition, no excuse for old shoes or a macaroni diet. We could have donated half to the United Way to help other kids, bought him a car when he turned sixteen, or put him in hockey gear for the next few years.

11. A Hypothetical Situation

Now that we are aware of what Parent Alienation is and what to do if it happens, it is easy to get carried away and point fingers every time a child cries. It is important to be mindful of each situation with your child and not jump to conclusions too quickly. For instance, what if your child cries when you drop them off at your ex's? Does this mean that they hate it there and are being abused? Most certainly not. It is common for a child to cry when being dropped off at another caregiver's place, daycare, or the other parent's house. This is what is called secure attachment. With a good caregiver, who will entertain the child and redirect them in a loving caring way, the cries usually dissipate fairly quickly. The child has an attachment to that parent at the time, but with a loving environment, the child feels safe and will continue having fun. This will change when they're with the other parent for a period of time.

I have found that dropping your child off at the other parent's house rather than having them picked up, if possible, gives them reassurance that it is ok. You're not leaving them, you're telling them it's ok to go. The best thing is for the parents to work together. Let the parent come in, engage in family things for a while, distract the child just as they would at daycare, and ease into the goodbye. This gives the child a short time to get some of the attachment to the other parent back.

Children have difficulty distinguishing time. A few days can seem like a long time for them, while a long stay can seem short. This is why it is important for both parents to follow roughly the same pattern at each house. When one parent lets the child stay up past bedtime and lets them do whatever they want all the time, this gives the child a false sense of life and rules. The child expects this at the other parent's house, and will start to get upset because it's not as fun there. This is an environment where Parent Alienation can start and become something horrible.

Imagine now that you're the custodial parent. You are angry because the other parent seems to make their visits a fun house with no rules. This makes it difficult for the custodial parent to get the child back into a routine.

Let's forget about the parents for just a minute and be mindful of what the child is experiencing emotionally. The child is upset with the custodial parent; they are most likely pouting, or reacting in a non-positive way, inviting feelings of anger, and confusion as to why it's so different, and the discomfort of a new routine. A child can learn to be in two different homes and maintain their happiness if the parents work together and keep a consistent, loving environment.

The non-custodial parent may be doing this out of spite, or simply because they only get two days every second weekend. Most likely, those two days are when they are off work and they only have a short time to catch up and spend some time with their child, naturally they want this time to be filled with fun - waterslides, parks, pizzas, and cartoons. So much to do and so little time. That parent sees nothing wrong with this. So what do the parents do? They start arguing their sides, and the anger builds and builds. This is when the parents need to sit down together and think about the best interests of the child. What solution could they possibly find when they are upset, arguing, and failing to see the other's point of view? By thinking about what the other parent is feeling and how both of their actions are affecting their child, at least there is a chance at a possible solution. Perhaps the custodial parent doesn't want the visits to be more than two days, or the non-custodial parent doesn't want to have them for more than two days.

Both parents need to compromise. The custodial parent gives one more day to the visits, making it three days. Two days on the parent's days off, as well as the Monday, so they can still have fun, but get the child back into a routine on Sunday for school or daycare on Monday morning. The non-custodial parent, may not be too happy because it will be difficult to get the child to daycare/school when they have to work, the custodial parent may not be happy because they are unsure if the other parent is ready and responsible enough for this,

However, good changes do start to happen. The non-custodial parent, after a month of seeing what it is like to have to worry about making lunches, bedtime, laundry and so on, starts appreciating what the other parent does every day. The bond with their child grows stronger in a different way; it's not just about having fun, but about real life as well.

The custodial parent, after getting used to the new schedule, is more comfortable with spending more time away from their child. Not only is their child happier coming back and in a routine, they are starting to see that the child is safe. Not to mention having time off from even a couple of school nights, lunches, laundry, baths, and so on, can be nice.

Even if the custody situation remained the same until the child turned eighteen, it would still be a beautiful change.

Korina's Story

After five years of what I believed to be a happy and successful relationship, my common-law husband left me for another woman. Our son was one and a half years old at the time. It was a very painful time in my life. I was devastated, extremely hurt and betrayed. Anger was an emotion that soon followed. Not only was I struggling to come to terms with the emotional pain of the end of my relationship but I was also adjusting to life as a single mom.

The struggle wasn't easy, but hating my ex was. I was so angry with him! How could he do this to us? To our family? To our son? At times, I thought he didn't even deserve to be a father. I viewed him as selfish and undeserving of a relationship with his son. At that point, he wasn't making much of an effort to even see his son, or his other children from his previous relationship. Let's just say he wasn't known to be the most experienced father and definitely wouldn't be getting any awards for the World's Greatest Dad! Yet, he was a father nonetheless. My son's father.

Unsure of how well he would care for him, and because he was living with the other woman, I did not want my son to have a relationship with someone who was a part of the destruction of our family. I felt uneasy allowing him to take our young son anywhere. I did offer for my ex to have supervised visits at my home, where I would go into another room, or at a park and I would sit in my car. This experience proved to be hard for me, as I am sure it was for him as well. Seeing him and watching him play with our son only hurt me more and was a constant reminder that we were no longer a family. To make matters worse, my ex was angry with me (due to the circumstances I'm sure). Every visit he had with his son was either preceded or followed by an argument between my ex and myself. Arguments about "us" and our relationship, which in all reality had nothing to do with our son or him being able to have a relationship with our son; the whole experience was unpleasant for all of us.

During this time, we had gone to a justice counselor to legalize our custody agreement and hopefully settle the issue out of court. I wanted sole custody and guardianship with supervised access, just as we had already been doing. He signed the papers and we agreed on a child support amount. (After this, the visits became fewer and far between). I was in disbelief that he didn't fight me on this. It almost made me angrier and I lost even more respect for him as a father, even though I ended up getting the arrangement I wanted.

At one point, a couple of months had passed without even a phone call or a visit from him. My heart was breaking for my little boy and, as easy as it was for me to move forward and not have to deal with or see my ex anymore, I had to put my own feelings aside and do what was best for my son. Every son needs a father; I knew that in the back of my mind. Let's face it; I wasn't exactly making it easy for my ex to have a quality relationship with his son. I wasn't even giving him a chance. At the time I thought I was being fair (you get what you give, after all), was I really though?

I decided to open an email account for my son, so they could at least communicate online and I could share photos of our son with him. I was doing something on my part but the rest was up to him. However, we still continued arguing but this time it was online through email. My ex sent me an email asking; why couldn't he just have his son visit him at home (where he was living with this other woman)? I sent a response back and my immediate answer was "No," I didn't even think about it. I let my anger lead. My ex of course, was very angry with me.

After a day of thinking about it, I realized who I was really hurting. I knew the answer and was shameful of it; I was hurting my son. I thought I was protecting him, but in the long run I was only hurting him. I had to move on and learn how to come to terms with all of it.

The circumstances were not what I would have chosen but it happened and I had to make a conscious decision to at least let him try to be a father and have a relationship with his son – one that wasn't just on my terms.

So I put my hurt and anger aside and called my ex to tell him that, after some thought, it would be okay for my son to visit him, to a point where we were both comfortable. I knew I didn't want to be a part of the reason why my son didn't have his father in his life.

I now regularly (every week) drop my son off and pick him up at my ex's. My son, who is now four, looks forward to going to his dad's every week. I realized that in letting go of my anger and hurt I have since been able to move on and have now become happy again. My ex and I can even talk about our son and make other small talk without arguments. In letting my anger go, he has also been able to put his anger aside for the best interest of a common goal, the happiness of our son.

Korina Macdonald

12. POWER STRUGGLE

Often the fighting between former partners is a fight for who holds the power. This can occur for a number of reasons. Let us look at the most common ones:

The parent with less time doesn't like the idea of being the inferior of the two, resulting in retaliation against the other parent.

The parent with the majority of the child's time is power tripping and exerts most of their energy making the other parent feel inferior. Nothing they do is good enough as they are only a part-time parent. Either way, the power struggle pushes on and unfortunately, the most effective way to punish the other parent and win that all-important power trip is to do so through the child.

When we break down this power struggle and start to see the emotions that go along with it, we immediately have to understand that, no matter what has happened, you share the child with someone else.

Some of the consequences of a power struggle are:

Anger: toward the other for being the cause of the situation.

Jealousy: because they have most of the power, or jealously because of their new partner.

Guilt: about not seeing the child and trying to make up for that in ways that don't benefit the child or situation, like letting them do things they are normally not allowed to do.

Money: hating the fact that money has to be paid, or on the other side, putting money ahead of what truly matters in another attempt to be the winner of the power struggle. Support is a given and if it has to be paid, then pay it. If you are the parent with the most access, don't make money the deciding factor on access issues. If there is a court order in place and they haven't paid, it will catch them. Family maintenance will garnish their wages or take their tax return and you will get a lump sum payment later. Your child does not care about money, only about seeing both their mom and dad.

So how do we stop this power struggle? We have to get to the root of our anger and fix it. We must see that what is truly important is the health and well-being of the child ahead of petty anger issues. No one likes to be dumped, but it is not the end of the world. In time, things will get easier and you can reflect back at how silly you may have acted. People in a shared access scenario seem to have it the best, there is no struggle for power and both sides are equal. Like children, when the blocks/toys are divided equally and they share, they stop fighting. Unfortunately, parents can rarely put the best interests of their child over the hatred they feel toward their ex. They live in the mentality of "I hate my ex more than I love my child." Some schedules are not about the best interest of the child at all, they simply place the percentage of time exactly where one parent gets full support payments. It's the "who has the most toys wins" concept.

You may feel guilty as a single parent so you try to give your children everything to compensate. The problem with "everything is about your kids," is that people can go too far. What happens is the opposite of what you're trying to achieve. There is a fine line between doing everything for your kids, and spoiling them to the point of no respect. Once your kids get used to this parenting strategy, your strategy of doing what you think is best for them backfires. Now all of a sudden you are dealing with kids who expect expensive gifts at Christmas, for example, and show attitude and disrespect when they get a less than expected birthday present. We need to understand that we may believe the kids aren't getting what they deserve in this new single parenting life, but we cannot try to compensate with letting them stay up, or spoiling them rotten. They will benefit from normal structure, bedtimes, birthdays, etcetera. A child who is given everything to make them happy can suffer from the same emotional trauma as abused children, because typically the parents substitute material things to make up for the lack of quality time spent with their children. This lack of time together can negatively affect the attachment the child has for their parents. It can affect the parts of the child's brain that deal with love, relationships, trust, and so on.

As much as it is about your kids, it is also about you, and although it is hard to see at the time, spoiling them is hurting all of you in the long run. Think about life with your kids if you were still with your partner. Your kids would still do fun things and be involved in extracurricular activities, but would they be staying up late, complaining about little things like crappy snacks and poor presents? What kids benefit from, in any relationship, is fun mixed with discipline, for without the rain, we wouldn't appreciate the sunshine.

How the "Power Struggle" directly affects your child:

Time away from the other parent. This gives the alienating parent time to turn the child against the other parent.

Feelings of abandonment. A child believes the parent doesn't love them or care to see them.

Parts of the brain that deal with love and affection, can be affected, possibly leading to a child being overly quiet, suffering from low self-esteem, depression or possibly suicidal.

The child's attachment to the parent starts to dissipate

Rules: As a part-time parent, perhaps you aren't enforcing the rules that need to be enforced, out of fear that if you have to punish your child, it will just add points to the other side because your house is no fun. The problem with this is that the child goes back to the other parent's house expecting things like late bedtime, ice cream for supper, or whatever it may be. This is just making things worse for the one of you who is doing what's best for the child! Now they are getting in trouble when they go back to the other parent's house, and only after a few days of routine again, do they realize that playing by the rules doesn't get them in trouble. What a torturous procedure to have to go through every time they see their mom or dad.

Fighting out of anger. Fighting with the child nearby will affect them greatly. Remember, you are both that child's role models. If you have to disagree, do it when your child is away from sight and sound.

Either we continue to sugar-coat it or we as parents are completely oblivious to the fact that fighting between parents is affecting the child emotionally. The one who wins the power struggle and gets the majority access wins, but it doesn't stop there. There is a continuous battle for further control; the other parent retaliates in hatred and now both parents are ignoring their child's needs completely, both physically and emotionally. In this never-ending power struggle, you wake up one day believing you're the victor, but will realize you have actually lost it all. Once a child loses attachment with a parent, they are headed down a steep and dangerous hill.

13. The Almighty Dollar

I took my son to an arcade where they have video games, bumper cars, mini golf, and ticket games, where you can win tickets to buy toys at their store. We had boatloads of fun. My son played all the big kid games and passed on the ticket games, which I tried to encourage, but he didn't want to. He played and just had fun. He didn't get the concept that more tickets equaled more stuff in the end. He would play big people games, pool, and even the broken game, with the old doll on strings; when you pushed a button, the doll's arms and legs were supposed to move about. The doll's face is something out of a horror show, creepy.

When it was time to go, I told him that he could a get a prize with the tickets, and his face lit up. He chose a sticky hand, you know those rubbery hands that you throw or flick and it sticks on things. On the way home, I was getting slapped in the face with this sticky hand while trying to drive. When we got home, he was slapping everything in the house. His laughter rang out even louder than before. Not only did he not get bored with this sticky hand, but also every slap made just increased his fun. He was absolutely devastated when, later, he couldn't find his sticky hand in the mess that, by both our faults, was his room.

Seeing that he was devastated, and I in a weird kind-of-way, was missing getting slapped with a sticky hand in the forehead with that distinct sound I'm sure only a sticky hand can make, went to the mall to buy him a new one. This way, when he was back with me, the pleasure would pick up where it had left off. I can assure you, it was for his pleasure, not for the pleasure of my forehead, or my sanity.

Wouldn't you know it; I couldn't find one anywhere, nowhere at all. Three hours later, I am in for ten dollars worth of gas and starting to think weird things.

So I do what I have to do and return to the arcade to buy a sticky hand. Well, I should have known that in my world things aren't so obvious or easy. You can't buy them; you have to win them with the fake money that you get for playing the games! So, I buy some tokens to simply win that sticky hand. Wouldn't you know it; I am horrible at these games. Looks easy, Whack the Mole, you ever heard of this game? You have to be a ninja! I smash away at these outdated brown things that look like poop popping out, and even if you are quick enough to hit them, they don't budge. So I two-hand the bonker and get serious; smashing away at this machine that now has "personal" written all over it. I am sweating and now people are starting to look. You have to remember I am here alone, no kids, just Jack Nicholson in the mansion losing his mind, swearing at these turd-like things they call moles, which apparently have superhuman strength (or super-mole strength). The worst part was forgetting that the bonker had a rope attached. So after my hand flew off the bonker, I was standing there, hitting hard turds with an imaginary bonker. I figured that, before I got locked up, I should move onto the next game. You may already know what happened next. I got sucked in, compelled, hypnotized if you will, by the old stupid, creepy dancing doll! I had to try to make it work, and it didn't – again! I grumbled and again, kids were running away from me and I was sure I was going to get kicked out and arrested at any moment.

Just then, my luck turned around. I saw a kid to my left in the ticket room winning all kinds of tickets on a game. I had no choice but to redeem myself and get the tickets for my son's sticky hand. I went up to the boy and begged him to let me in on his secret. He did, but I was out of tokens. So back to the line-up again I went to purchase a couple more tokens.

When I got back, there was a line for the game, of course. So after about thirty minutes thinking about how great a parent I am, yet at the same time wanting to play Whack A Turd, I was told by these kids to stand back and wait my turn. After a short but seemingly lifetime's wait, I plunge all of my hard-earned tokens into this game, and sure enough, out come the tickets. Well, I tell you the joy of the tickets coming out was such a relief, I threw my hands in the air and shouted like I was at the casino and had won! Again, people were looking, and I wasn't sure why. I thought perhaps they were jealous, until I went to cash my tickets in. I walked up to the counter with my handful of tickets and threw them in the plastic bin like I was going all in. They gave me my cash to spend at the store. I, for once in my life, felt rich – with only a handful of bills! Of course, I got excited, wanting to buy the whole store and a round for the people behind me. That was before the nice thirteen-year-old attendant pointed out that the bills were only worth about fifty dollars and, wouldn't you know it, the sticky hand was thirty dollars. Add two candies and I was broke. Story of my life!

Do you think my son cared how much the sticky hand cost? Will he ever know what I went through to get it? Maybe one day, but by then, he will have different worries like getting his driver's license. The sticky hand cost me thirty times what it was worth but my son didn't know any better or any worse. He didn't know what a dollar was, or how much things cost. He just knew that he had fun with it.

It doesn't matter to kids what they have. It could be a sticky hand or a new dirt bike. You don't have to buy their love and they sure don't care about money issues between Mom and Dad.

14. TRUTH

Your children do not always need to know the truth. Now don't get all excited and get your feathers ruffled, what I mean by this is, do we really understand what the difference between truth and perception, as well as the difference between fact and opinion, really is?

Perhaps your ex cheated on you, maybe he or she is lazy, maybe your ex is an inconsiderate $/%*&! Maybe your ex-husband sleeps with everything he sees, or your ex-wife is a bar star. Maybe your ex is selfish and is too involved in his work to care about the kids' soccer games. Maybe your ex is self-centered and worried about her nail appointments rather than your daughter's gymnastics class. He may be a bad husband or boyfriend and she may be a bad wife or girlfriend; however, that does not mean that they are bad parents.

Even if these things are true, they are none of your child's business. These are your perceptions and opinions of them and it is unfair to pass them on to your child. Just as you have opinions about them, they have opinions about you. Is it the truth? Perhaps, to a certain degree, but what triggers their actions? Do all people feel this way about them? Probably not. You and your friends do, and vice versa. It is not up to one parent to tarnish the other parent. When it comes to talking with your children, all, and I mean all, negative comments are not to be said aloud. What is your self-image? Is it the same as your ex's or the same as all your workmates? Most definitely not, the truth is what we perceive it to be and unless there is evidence, it is merely an opinion. What the mother and father perceive about each other after a relationship is quite different from when they were happy during the relationship.

Let's look at it from a child's point of view, shall we? They know they love mom and dad, and as they get older they start to learn how mom and dad created them out of love. Now one of the parents starts the hate game, how confusing! Your child is thinking, "You want me to hate someone you created me out of love with?"

How could this possibly make sense to a child? Is it really worth tormenting the child and run the risk of damaging your child forever, affecting who they will become as an adult just to win a hate war against your ex? Hurting the very child to whom you also teach love and sharing, all because of your opinion.

What we think, or more specifically are told, becomes our truth, right or wrong. Truth, when mixed with our perceptions, can become convoluted as we shamelessly distort it to suit ourselves. Sometimes our truths are nothing more than opinions or perceptions.

THE DIFFERENCE BETWEEN TRUTH AND PERCEPTION IS A SPACE THAT NO ONE LOOKS INTO. ALL CHOOSE A SIDE, AND THEN CHOOSE TO DENY ALL THAT IS NOT ALIGNED, EACH TO ITS OWN LIE.

Unknown

15. A Child's Best Interests

Children do not always want what is best for them. What they say they want is not always what they truly want. And they do not always say what they truly want.

Dr. Richard Warshak

You were probably in your lawyer's office when you first heard the phrase, "The best interests of your child." What does this really mean? This term or phrase, "In the child's best interest" has become nothing more than a "How are you?" or, "I'll call you sometime," Just conversation to take up time and be polite. I am sure the first time we heard the phrase, instead of thinking about what it truly means, we just put it in front of our unchanged thoughts and unrealistic ideas of what is best for our child because of our hatred-induced tantrums. This phrase, "in the child's best interest" transforms a thought like "They don't deserve to see the kids" into "It is not in my child's best interest to be with them." Instead of thinking about what this phrase really means, we just use it as an excuse.

I do not have an official definition on what the best interests of a child are, because it changes from child to child and from situation to situation. I will, however, give you a glimpse of my hard work and research to help you determine if something really is in your child's best interest. Please feel free to copy this list and use in the future. Perhaps put it on your fridge.

It MAY NOT be in your child's best interests:

- If you limit or disallow access to the other parent based simply on your hatred toward the other parent.

- If you tell lies to make your child dislike the other parent, their house, their dog, etcetera.

- If you encourage them to misbehave.

- If you teach them that your religion is good and the other parent's religion is bad.

- If you tell them they don't have to take their personal safety into account – like skateboarding without a helmet.

- If you compare their achievements to other children in a negative way.

- If you encourage them to climb onto the roof to overcome their fear of heights.

- If you go to the zoo and want them to stand inside the polar bear exhibit to take a photo.

- If you leave your TV on all night so you don't have to get up with the kids in the   morning.

- If you get them to stand with an apple on their head and urge them not to move ...because you want to try out your new bow and arrow.

A child's best interests, now who really knows what this means? How many parents really truly know and practice this? I feel compelled to clear this up because I think we, as parents, misread the phrase and think it says "The best interests of me, me and ONLY ME!" or that it means, "As long as the other parent is miserable, stressed out, and broke; then I have won and I am now happy." This behaviour is, I would say, childish. One can see that this type of behaviour is destined to do the opposite. While you think it is making you happy it is simply destroying your child, slowly but surely, like maggots getting rid of an animal carcass.

For example, your child should go to bed at 8.00 pm but you think that you will let them stay up a bit later, just so you're more 'fun' than you ex; or you know you should feed them a healthy lunch, but instead you give them junk food because you know it's what they would prefer and would make the other parent angry.

This kind of "angry parenting" offers zero benefits to your child. Perhaps it makes you feel better; maybe the child will go back and hate their other parent because they don't get ice cream at 9:30 pm. Congratulations, the child hates the other parent's house. You feel good, but the court order still stays the same, they still have to go to your ex's house. You do not see how hard it is on your children; they argue with their parent, because they expect life to be consistent, they expect the later bedtime and junk food for supper. When they don't get it, they act up and that results in punishment of some sort and everyone is stressed.

If you think that what is best for your child is punishment and stress, then maybe you need to take additional parenting courses, or an anger management course. There are more people being hurt here than just you!

I have heard of parents who refuse to give the other parent a copy of report cards. If that child lives with you fulltime and the other parent requests a copy of the report card, then send them a copy of the report card! Are you punishing the parent or the child? It's the child who gets punished when they aren't allowed to hear both their parents say, "I am proud of you," upon seeing their grades. Do you think the other parent doesn't still think about their child? Do you think the child doesn't still think about them?

Close your eyes and picture this. You are at work and you get a phone call from the hospital. They tell you that your child was seriously injured in an accident and you are needed at the hospital as soon as possible. What goes through your head? Your child's safety. Why does that get ignored in these break-up fights? Forget about the anger and jealousy and think about the best interests of your child.

Now, I'm not saying that we are responsible for everything our children do. Kids have their own minds and can think for themselves. All I am saying is that if you kick a dog every time they urinate on the carpet, you can hardly blame them for doing it on the hardwood floor.

My ex once claimed that it wasn't in our son's best interest to be away from her for more than two nights. She claimed it was because he suffers from hyperactivity and has high levels of anxiety when over-stimulated (this is another example of people saying whatever they want in court). It was so ridiculous that I didn't even bother getting him assessed by a professional. I assumed that if there were any concerns about this condition, it would have already been assessed. (If you truly had a concern for your child, you would have dealt with it then). Eventually, my son was with me for a whole week. He attended his new daycare and adjusted beautifully like nothing was off. He made friends and didn't want to leave when he was picked up. The daycare said he fit in just fine. So you see, people say these things but not out of the best interest of their child. These things are in the best interests of their hatred and drive to punish the other parent. Rather than keep fighting about it, let's break it down.

16. THE VICTORY OF THE LAST NAME

This is not a competition. Do not fight just to ensure your child's name is exactly the same as yours. A lot of children have both last names included in their name. I, for example, am a Greckul by birth. I was turned into a Williams because I was young when my mom got married and I didn't get a say in what my last name would be.

Some people take a child's last name so personally, saying for example, "he/she will never be a Williams," forgetting there are two parents and whose surname the child takes is not the ultimate prize. Maybe the father/mother is never around, or abusive, etcetera, and you have nothing to do with them. The last name still isn't the major issue. So change the name, get mad that they don't have your name, but never deny them their family heritage. One day, whether they have your ex's last name or not, their family history could be crucial to their health. Eventually, a doctor will ask your child, about their family's medical history; "Did your dad/mom have high blood pressure? Did they have cancer, diabetes, asthma, etcetera?" How are we, as adults, supposed to know these things when we have no idea of the family history? There are bigger issues surrounding family than just a last name, focus on the bigger picture and let the last name slide.

17. Religion

There is only one way to deal with religion in a break-up, and that is by doing what is in the best interest of the child involved. There are simple ways to deal with religious differences; but all too often, each side is just too much about themselves and not about their child.

Keep in mind that our job as parents is to raise our children to the best of our ability, providing them with a wholesome loving environment, protection, food, shelter, and, of course, you will teach them what you believe in, and what you perceive to be right. This does not mean that the other parent who grew up differently is wrong, they just have a different perception on life and that is okay. That is how we enjoy different cultures, different foods, I could go on and on. In a situation where there is a break-up, you as a parent are still responsible for teaching your child these things. Separated parents, however, take this to a whole new level. They feel that it is necessary not only to teach their child their beliefs and perceptions, but also what is wrong with the other parent's beliefs and perceptions. Of course I say this, and everything in this book, on the basis that this is a relationship where there are two capable parents. I'm not applying this to a situation like telling your child that drugs, abuse, and so on, at the other parent's house are wrong. This is about the esoteric things, about perceptions and beliefs.

In a split situation, your job is to live life as normally as you can with no pressure on the child, to teach them what you believe and leave it at that. The other parent will teach them what they believe, or how they were raised, and not what is wrong at the other parent's house. When, and if, the child asks why there is a difference, that's when it is up to the parents to work together on the same page. If working from the same hymn sheet so to speak, isn't possible, simply tell the child that this is how things are at Mom's house, because that is what Mom believes, and things are done differently at Dad's house because his beliefs are different than Mom's. And that is OK!

If you both have the same religion, then life is good; you may not realize how good. If one person has a particular faith and the other follows none at all, then the answer is relatively simple. The parent with a particular faith teaches the child what they believe to be true, and leaves it at that. Do not tell your child that the other is wrong as this just confuses them unnecessarily. If they ask, your answer should be that they need to talk about it with their other parent. If you are the parent that does not have faith, then your job is to simply say that you do things differently, not teach your children to dislike the other's faith. You may not attend church, but they can go with the other parent when they return .

If you both have different faiths, or since the break-up, have entered into a different one, then it can get tricky and ugly. The fight back and forth turns into hatred and increases the tension between everyone, especially the children, who are now turned into soldiers.

Interrogated when they get back, tortured until they tell the awful truth of whether they went to church, and that it is wrong to go there and believe that nonsense. There will be no fun, soldier! First, the brainwashing must commence – Got It? It is bad there, it is good here, they are wrong, do not believe them; believe me because I love you! I will protect you they will not! OK good, so how was it at Dad's/Mom's house? Did you have fun? Did they take you to church? Their church is wrong; you know that right? The soldier weakens, and retreats away from all of this confusion. All they wanted was to see the other parent and now they feel bad. They don't know why they should feel bad, they only love their parents. The soldier slowly gets distant from the leaders, eventually seeking refuge in some other commander, perhaps an aunt or uncle, maybe a family friend – someone who doesn't interrogate or torture them. Both commanders have lost the battle, but the war for the soldier is far from over. The war has become theirs, and even if they are triumphant in the end, they still lose.

As complicated, twisted, and disgusting as these types of situations become, again, there is a relatively simple answer. Teach your own beliefs and don't talk negatively about theirs. Why is that so hard? Because each parent gets so infuriated that the other is teaching the child something different! The only, and I repeat only, way to raise your child to be a sane individual, and for them perhaps to end up believing in God at all, is to teach them about your religion, but not at the expense of the other parent. When asked why you go to one church and the other parent goes to another one, just tell them it's ok that you go to different churches and believe different things. When they are older, they will choose for themselves which faith (if any), they want to enter into. Hopefully, the parents haven't driven them too far away from God by then.

The best answer I have ever heard to the battle of religion and the age-old question of what came first, the chicken or the egg came from an egg farmer from TLC's hit TV show, "Dirty Jobs," with Mike Rowe. At the end of the show, Mike asked the farmer what came first, "the chicken or the egg?" The farmer replied with the perfect answer, which in my opinion stops the fight between the two sides. He said, "If you believe in God and

Creationism, the answer is chicken, as he created animals first. If you don't believe in God and Creation, then you believe in Evolution, which would suggest that we evolved from a cell then to an egg, so the answer is egg." Plain and simple. Believe what you believe, while having respect for others who may not think the way you do.

18. Involvement Of Ex's Parents

Excerpt from my Journal:

December 4, '09

Three days after my 31st birthday and one day before my first court appearance. I am outside and the snow has just started to fall. With all of the stress I have been enduring, I am surprisingly calm. There has always been something calming about a snowfall for me. Maybe it is because I am a December baby; I'm not sure. I tilt my head back like a Pez dispenser and just watch it fall in a calm quiet way.

Some people think negatively as soon as the snow starts falling. Anger, fear, or anxiety set in, as they think about the shoveling, the driving, or the tacky winter boots that don't match anything in the closet. I have even heard radio ads about the epidemic of injured postal workers slipping on the icy driveways and sidewalks. Insurance companies are flooded with insurance claims from accidents, yet I gaze up into the star-like flurry with the utmost peace. How can you be anything but mesmerized by something that is so small, there are so many of them but no two are exactly alike. Each flake is unlike the next, some big ones, some small ones, but most are the same size. Even though every one of these intricate flakes is different and they fall in a scattered pattern with no rhyme or reason, like a leaf in a windstorm, they are calming. For the same reason, I guess, that butterflies are calming and peaceful.

People enjoy butterflies and their beauty. Even though a butterfly flies with the most erratic and unusual flight plan, when it lands, its beauty is most appreciated and calming. You may only have a brief moment to stare at the beauty before it takes off again in its unusual and irregular pattern that seems to lack uniformity and grace. I watch the snow fall in this same pattern and try to catch a snowflake on my tongue; their sporadic movements make it difficult and also quite a victory. I watch how they land, and even though every one is intricate and diverse, they all seem to start fitting together. Each one compliments the next. This complex puzzle, consisting of trillions of intricate and unique puzzle pieces, continues to fit together creating the most even blanket of snow and yet versatile enough to fit together if packed into a snowball. I think of how, between snowfalls, there are distinct layers created and if you look at the side of a big snow bank when some of it falls away, you can still see the layers of each snowfall. You can see where, over time, the layers have been created at different times and temperatures, making me wonder how they can continue to grow and layer, still working together. Each of us is different, and we should be working together like the snowflakes. Even though each of us is different and unique, we can all fit together to create a balance, a blanket of snow, so to speak, that all fits together.

They say that apples can't be compared to oranges, so maybe butterflies can't be compared to snowflakes. I think they can though, because if we look hard enough, we can definitely see similarities between so-called opposites like these. Apples and oranges are fruits; they have seeds. Butterflies and snowflakes are both beautiful and move in an irregular, yet graceful pattern. People are the same and the layers, over time, suggest that as we each belong to different generations, we need to understand each other. We can learn from one another and build a bond so strong that these layers will not slip. Accept old ideas and new, young and old, while creating layers that will not slip but continue to grow and be strong, contributing to create a most symbiotic relationship.

Grandparents that step into any divorce or break-up should proceed with caution. Your grandchildren need you in their life; they always have and always will, but be there for them with love. Do not join in on the Parent Alienation. We have learned a lot from you, yes, but our children need to learn from the next generation as well. Somehow, all generations need to learn to understand each other better, and learn from them, the old to the young, and the young to the old. Times change, situations change and a mix of parenting styles from different generations are better than one firm opinion. Our children don't benefit from being on the computer all day and they are hardly going to walk uphill both ways to school in -40 degree weather carrying a frozen backpack.

Grandparents, if you are giving your son or daughter advice on parenting, then do so in love and understanding, and with the knowledge that times are changing. Mom isn't home all day with the kids, cleaning, and making supper while Dad is off working to support the family. The jalopy doesn't cost $100 anymore and the stressful days of gas going up to five cents a gallon are over. It takes two people to make life and bills work. For the parents who are doing it on their own, God bless their hearts, it is difficult. The single parent lifestyle is becoming the norm these days and is hard on everyone, especially the children.

19. STEPPARENTS

Stepparents can be a wonderful addition to a struggling family; however, they can also bring the final blows of an emotional wrecking ball that could leave your children crumbling, falling, and landing on the ground, in an unseen dust cloud of negative and hateful feelings.

If you are the one entering a single parent's life, listen up. You are the one entering the children's lives; the children are not entering yours. They didn't choose you, the situation was chosen for them by you and their parent. You are walking into an already established family. There are different types of families, and even though they are different, they are still an established family with established rules. Don't try to change that.

Your stepchildren may be glad to have you in their life, or they may hate you, thinking that you are trying to replace their mother or father. Regardless, you are the one who came into their lives and they have the right to accept you or turn you away.

As stepparents, you need to let the children know that you are not there to turn their lives upside down or change everything. Rather, you should let them know that you are genuinely there for them, and truly have their best interests at heart. They need to know that their best interests are still going to be looked after, even with you in the picture. If you agree with Maslow's Hierarchy of Needs theory, the child's top two needs must to be looked after before they can move on to the next. Only then will they be able to grow and open up.

This means enduring the possible negative responses from the children: the "I hate you, you're not my mom or dad,"; "Mom would let me," or "Dad would say it's ok." Showing love, time after time, is the only way to eventually to show them that you are there for them, getting upset at them and punishing them is not going to help your case in any way.

As a new boyfriend or girlfriend, husband or wife, you may feel compelled to stick up for your new partner, getting involved in pushing the other parent away, saying things like, "We are happy now" or "We are a family now and you should just go away." Don't join in on the alienation. You are only getting one side of the story, and even if it is somewhat true, neither the maternal parent nor the stepparent, have the right to alienate the child.

So how do you let your stepchildren know that they cannot beat you around like a piñata, but at the same time let them know that you are there for them? Time, a lot of time. Here are a few hints that may help:

Show them constant love and understanding.

Empathize with them and their situation. Don't try to get them to empathize with yours.

Understand that you will be the outsider coming in and it will take time (sometimes a lot of it) to show them that you are good for them and that you aren't leaving.

Do not engage in any battles against the mother or father, or voice negative thoughts and/or opinions.

Do not expect the children just to forget about their birth parents and call you Mom or Dad.

If you think you are ready to accept the children and treat them as your own, while at the same time understanding they have a mother and father and you are not there to take that away from them; if you understand that you may have work a little harder and bend a little more, then you're on the right track. This just might work for you and your new family. If, however, this seems like more than you are interested in or capable of handling, think twice before you proceed. This is not in the best interests of you, the biological parent, and most importantly, the children, who have been through enough trauma by this point.

Why are we taught not to compare apples with oranges? Why are we taught to look past the similarities? In explaining comparisons to people, I often compare such things like snowflakes and butterflies. Perhaps what we are missing is the ability to make the connection between what is similar, rather than focus on what is so different. We may just find as many, or even more similarities, than differences. Apples and oranges both contain seeds, are fruits and both grow on trees. They both contain vitamin c and fiber. They are round in shape, make juice, and are easily packed in lunches. I wonder what similarities we could find between love and hate.

20. Love and Hate

What are love and hate, and how are they similar? Love, we could say, is the ultimate dedication to someone, to want to fulfill their every need because it truly makes you happy. So much so that you would even give your life for them, or at least a kidney. Hate equally consumes you and you could end up giving your life for someone or something because you hate it that much. Maybe it's a life of drinking and drugs. For some, it is suicide, but sometimes not before taking others with you, children included. For some, it may be a life in prison because of acting out on extreme feelings of hate. Love can also consume and make people act unusually, perhaps violently, and vindictively. Hate, at first glance, is what makes people hurt the ones they love, but is it because of love or because of hate? Would we hate so much if love wasn't there? They feed off each other. Without hate, you could not have love, because you quite simply cannot hate something that doesn't matter to you. You cannot possibly love something you hate either, so do you love them or hate them?

We love our children, so we hate our ex.

We love time with friends and family, so we hate our jobs.

We love to have a few drinks on Super Bowl Sunday, so we hate Monday morning.

A fire needs the correct environment to thrive, a combination of fuel to burn, and oxygen to feed it. If you take one of them out of the equation, the fire has no choice but to go out.

The difference between love and hate is that love will empower you; hate will consume you. Even though they seem to feed off each other, it is hate that needs love to survive. Love will thrive and continue to grow when thoughts of hate are no more. Love doesn't need hate to survive. Like the fire without oxygen, if we take out one component, hate, the only possible thing left to survive and thrive, is love.

As parents, I encourage you to think about the relationship between love and hate, and realize that we can, and must, get rid of one of them (of course I mean hate). If we don't, they will continue to feed off each other, and remain in our thoughts and actions, when what we should be doing is what's best for our children.

LOVE ME OR HATE ME, THEY'RE BOTH IN MY FAVOUR. IF YOU LOVE ME I WILL ALWAYS BE IN YOUR HEART. IF YOU HATE ME I WILL ALWAYS BE ON YOUR MIND.
Shakespeare

21. OUR CHILDREN ARE PUNISHED BY OUR STRESS

I f you think stress does not bother you or affect your life, if you think you can handle stress well and it does not affect the people around you, think again.

Excerpt from my Journal:

November 30, '09

The day before my 31st Birthday. It's supposed to be a happy day. I got my paycheck today. It was a lot less because of my lawyer bills, and I've helped pay for my older son's out of town hockey tournament. My car payment is coming out on the first. My phone is getting cut off on the 1st and my rent is $650.00. My check was $610.05. I've managed to beg and borrow money from friends to cover my payments. After all, how can I pay my lawyer if I don't have a phone? My heart is racing again, I'm always thinking about how I am going to be in contact with my lawyer and my son's mom for pickups and drop offs. I guess I could leave my work number with them. I am still $100 short on my rent and unable to buy groceries.

December 1st, My Birthday

I received a call from my lawyer, two days before court. His mom has filed an affidavit that was filled with more lies than a donkey farm has Hee Haws and, there were a whole lot of "Why I Oughta's" floating around. Are the courts this naive? Can someone really just make accusations and it is up to you to defend yourself? Right now, it feels like the answer is yes, but in all fairness, after the court process, I learned that most of the bitter lies and nonsense are seen by the judge as just that, lies.

If the lies work against us, and win, it will be painful for a long time. I continue to push ahead though; because I know when he's older he will ask questions. Questions like the ones I asked my dad; "Why? Where were you? Why did you leave me? Why didn't you love me?" I will be able to tell my son that I did everything in my power to fight for him, and who knows, maybe my book will be a success and he will read it someday. In any case, I can sleep at night knowing I didn't just stand by. I fought with everything I had because I love him!

I feel like giving up and just hope, like my dad did, that when my son's older, he will know the truth. However, it is not in me to give up on what I believe and I will continue through this insanity until the end, no matter what the outcome. Right now, my three-year-old hates me, his brother, and even the family dog. This is what keeps me going, saving him from emotional abuse.

Remember, the child doesn't hate you, the other parent does.

I am finding it hard to think positive when I hate her so much. Every new lie is a new blade (one of those self-sharpening ones that gets sharper when it enters and exits your back). I am trying to just forget it and be happy for the boys. When the boys and I are together, all my mind, thinks about is: "Why is she doing this? I hate her. NO, I don't hate her; I hate what she is doing." All I can do is take what I learned from when I went through this with my older son years ago, and use what I have learned in books and courses I have taken regarding Parent Alienation. I continue not to mention her or her house in a bad way and just have fun at my house and show constant love and affection.

What makes it gut wrenching is when he says things like, "I don't like this house," or "I don't like you," and hates everything fun that we used to do. I suck it up and all I reply is, "Daddy and your brother love you very much, and Mommy does things differently than Daddy. Mommy likes different things than Daddy, and Daddy likes things Mommy may not. Mommy goes to this church and Daddy goes to that church, and that's okay."

Two days before court and the lies on my ex's part are running rampant. My friend calls me at almost 10.00 p.m.; it was so nice to hear from a good friend in such a grief-stricken time for us. My elder son is still awake, which bugs me a little because he knows his bedtime on a school night is 9.00 p.m. I let him stay up, as I am excited for my phone call, to vent to someone, to help me get some stuff off my chest. I am on the phone to my friend. "How was your birthday?" she asks. "Well, I spent my birthday talking with my lawyer." I talk to my friend and it helps me to vent. It helps to complain to someone who understands and it makes me feel a little better knowing other people know the truth and that they are on my side.

Just when our conversation is getting good, my cordless phone starts to beep saying the battery is dying. I frantically run to my son's room, where the charger is, and go to grab the newly charged phone that is supposed to be there, and replace it with the dead phone to recharge it, a simple concept really. The phone is not there! I look around but the room seems to spin, like in the movies when someone loses their child in a busy mall. I finally find it is on his bed. I grab it in desperation to save the conversation, but it too, is dead. At this moment in time, this is devastating; I get angry and blame him for not charging the phone, which is totally out of character for me. He replies that he's not the only one who can hang up a phone, that he is not the only one responsible for making sure the two phones are charged; that there are two of us and it is both our responsibility. True and rational, but not what I want to hear at that moment; I look down at my arm and I don't yell or raise my voice, but my anger still gets the better of me and I throw the phone in the direction of the charger, hitting the wall before it lands on the counter.

The only person to converse with me, other than my lawyer, about all that has been going on, someone who understands, gets cut off because both of our phones are dead. It was his fault; it had to be. I wouldn't do such a thing in my time of stress and take temporary leave from my rational and clear mind. I take a breath, look at my son, and I apologize for my outburst. However, I sternly reinforce the fact that there are two phones in the house and there is no reason for both of them to be dead! He says that he's sorry too.

I'm writing this at 11.00 p.m. I tried going to sleep but my heart is pounding. I close my eyes and all I see is my two boys having fun, playing hockey. Then I see my younger son saying, that he doesn't like hockey and doesn't like this and that at Dad's house. I open my eyes, and look at the clock.

It is now 12.17 a.m. I spend the next hour thinking about my upcoming court appearance and then decide I should try to sleep, as I have to work at 7.00 a.m. the next morning. First, I must make some notes for my lawyer. I try to find a paper I had titled "notes for my lawyer" that I have been putting my last minute questions on. It has disappeared and my anger starts building again. Where did I put it; did my son touch it? I finally find the sheet of paper but it is ripped in two and one half is missing. I know I didn't rip it in half. Either I am really losing my mind or my son, for some unknown reason, my son has done this. He will hear about it tomorrow! I am furious; doesn't he realize how much stress I am under? How important that sheet is to me? I make additional notes then head off to bed.

When I enter my bedroom, I notice something on my bed that I didn't put there. The thoughts start racing again! What would he leave on my bed now? It is a bag; I grab it and look inside. There is a half-torn piece of paper on top of a box. It is my court paper! Confused, I flip it over and it reads: "Happy Birthday Dad, I love you." I open the box and it is a new set of kitchen knives and a cutting board. I had been complaining for months about having dull knives and nothing to chop food on. These knives are of high quality and I have no idea how he bought these. He has been babysitting for his aunty the last couple of weeks. Did he really spend all that money on knives for my birthday?

Have you ever heard the saying, "it could always be worse?" Well I singlehandedly demoted myself from being at the bottom of the emotional barrel, to digging a little deeper and further down.

"The difference between a rut and a grave is the depth" - Gerald Burrill

I am not like this, not ever! I want to wake him up and say I am sorry, but I can't, he has school tomorrow. I am crying and I want him to know that I did not mean to get that angry. I want him to know that I love him with everything my heart has.

"No, I am not stressed," I say to friends and co-workers. They all say they don't know how I do it. I hear them say things like "he's going through all the stress with his children and he always stays positive and funny." Yeah, real funny. Behind the scenes, I am a mess, a complete and total mess. I am the dirty water and grime spinning toward the drain of the tub, waiting to go down even further.

I hate her for doing this to me, to us. I keep using the word hate because it is the strongest adjective I have for her right now. I know it's not right. Perhaps I dislike her a little; perhaps I shouldn't let her get to me like this. Perhaps I can think what I want and I think I hate her. No, I don't hate anything or anyone, and even if I did, it doesn't mean I need to soak it in like a virus and spread it abroad. I don't hate her; I dislike what she is doing.

In any case, I cannot blame her for how I am acting – shame on me!

I look at the clock and it is now 1.17 a.m. My mind has taken a little break from thinking about court and lawyers, only to be replaced by the horrible guilt I feel for snapping at my boy, then finding his hard-worked-for birthday present on my bed. What do I say to him tomorrow? Nothing is a good enough excuse; nothing is justified. I hope he will understand and accept a good ol'fashioned "sorry." I will be at work when he leaves for school so I won't be able to talk to him until after.

It is 2.30 a.m. I am calling in sick for work tomorrow. I cannot afford to miss a day with my bills and Christmas coming up, but I cannot afford to lose my son's respect and leave his feelings hurt either. I will talk to him in the morning. In case he rushes out in the morning, I left him a note in the bathroom. The note read:

Son,

It's 2.30 a.m. and I still can't sleep. I feel horrible about taking the phone thing out on you. I was home all day and the phones were on the table, I could have put them on the charger. I AM TRUELY SORRY, BUD. I guess this court situation is getting to me more than I thought and I am sorry. I love you and I got your present, thank you! I don't know how you did it but you obviously worked hard at it. I love you so much and I am sorry, from today on I will not let any stress affect you...us, ok?

Please wake me up before you go to school if I am still sleeping, I called in sick but I need to hug you and assure you that I will be here for you, to let you know how badly I feel for last night. I love you bud.

I love you

Dad

My son did not hug me in the morning.

No matter how "cool as a cucumber" we think we are (I don't know where this saying came from but I'll "Google it" and get back to you), in this type of battle we are ALL riddled with stress, and it is impossible for it not to affect our children, even if we think we are hiding it. Even if we don't see it, we are slowly going crazy and are unaware that those around us cannot only see it, but feel it as well, like the hug from my son that next morning, neither seen nor felt. Let us make our children more cheerful and less tearful.

22. IALAC

I Am Loveable And Capable

The IALAC[1] story suggests that any child in any situation should be able to start their day wearing a sign that says "I Am Loveable And Capable." Everything thereafter—negativity, hurtful words and so on—all destroy this sign, one rip at a time. In essence, it destroys the child's self-esteem.

The story goes something like this:

Jayden, age 11, woke up one school morning and looked at his pajama top. He saw a neon sign. It flashed on and off, IALAC. Jayden knew at once that this meant "I Am Loveable and Capable." He dressed and went off to the kitchen. He was looking forward to his day.

---

[1] *I Am Loveable and Capable: A Modern Allegory on the Classical Put-Down*, Dr. Sidney B. Simon, University of Massachusetts Professor Emeritus (Retired)

Before Jayden could speak, his sister, Jordan, said, "You dummy! (rip off a corner of the sign) what did you do with my jacket?"

"Nothing," Jayden said. "Man," whined Molly, you're such a dork." (rip)

"Jayden, where is your backpack?" asked his mom.

"Oh no, I left it at school," said Jayden.

"Jayden," said his unhappy mother, "Why can't you use your brain?" (rip)

"But Mom,"Jayden said "I...."

"Don't talk back," said his mom. "You are such a smart mouth." (rip)

Jayden saw his sister smirking and whispering "Smart mouth." (double rip)

By the time Jayden left for the school bus, half of the IALAC was ripped.

On the bus, Missy Burns said, "Jayden you're dumb (rip) and a cry baby." (rip) Jenna, who Jayden thought was his best friend, laughed each time. (triple rip)

In the first period, Mrs. Fischer asked Jayden to put a homework problem on the board. Jayden forgot a division sign in the formula. "Jayden," Mrs. Fischer moaned, "how can you be so careless? I've told you a thousand times." (rip)

In language arts, Mr. Thomas barked at Jayden for getting the lowest score on the vocabulary quiz. (rip)

By the end of the day, Jayden went home with a very small IALAC sign. He was very upset.

The next day, Jayden woke up to find IALAC on his pajamas, but it was very small. He hoped today would be better. He wanted to keep his IALAC so much.

Try making a list of what you can do or say to increase your child's sense of IALAC.

I DON'T CARE WHO I LIVE WITH. I LOVE YOU BOTH. PLEASE DON'T MAKE ME CHOOSE — JUST TELL ME.

Nine year old boy

92

23. Three Bad Things Can Erase 10,000 Good Things

When this book was nearly done, I had a shocking conversation with my thirteen-year-old son. He was doing the dishes and couldn't fit a pot in the cupboard. I heard smashing, banging, and clanging coming from the kitchen.

I came into the kitchen and said, "Hey, what's going on?"

"I couldn't fit the pot in," he replied.

"So, that doesn't mean you have to throw everything. Take a breath and figure it out," I said.

It appeared that something else was bothering him and he didn't really want to talk about it. "Girlfriend stuff," he said.

"Fine, girls are a problem, but really, why so angry?" I asked. He said it was just a bad day. I bugged and bugged. I turned off his computer and said, "Let's talk."

What came out was something I couldn't have been less prepared for. He talked about how I always snapped and got angry, how I made him feel bad all the time. In my mind, I was the alienated parent who was doing the best I could. I had been protecting him from bad experiences and negativity only to find out, thirteen years later, that from his point of view I was doing the opposite. I mean, he wasn't around his mom anymore and we were happy. What was the problem? I thought life after that was great, that I did a great job. Apparently not, I could count on one hand the number of times I remembered getting angry around him and after all these years, that's what he remembers the most clearly. The number of good times, fun, birthday parties, hockey - all forgotten about; replaced instead, by three memories of me being angry with his alienating mother. More memories for him to hold in and act out in different ways and here I was unable to remember those three times, but at thirteen years old, they were as clear as day for him. Perhaps some memories were amplified by his alienating mother, but what's important was that he remembered my three outbursts which equalled to him, a parent who was always angry, and that's what he learned. Imagine that, 10,000 good memories all erased, or negatively influenced, by just three bad ones. Shame on me.

24. REMEMBERING YOUR OLDER KIDS

If you are going through a break-up, you may have a child from a previous relationship and are now dealing with another separation involving your second child. In this type of situation, you have a child who has already been through all of the horrible, parent-inflicted stress, and they are now looking at Round Two with apprehension. They know this will affect them again, because they were once the child who was ignored. When they were going through this, no one else saw the emotional abuse they were forced to deal with.

My elder son has been through some of the worst emotional trauma himself, and now he has to stand by, in anger, and watch his little brother getting lied to and ripped away from him. The sadness and anger in his heart are enough to fill our local pool and he still is expected by his teachers to continue his focus and grades in school. Can you imagine? Look at the stress that we, as adults, go through. It shows in our work habits and relationships and we still expect young kids and teens to sail smoothly through this! We have to consider them in this equation as well; they will also suffer through another nightmare as their younger sibling suffers through that same nightmare for the first time.

Raising a teenager can be stressful, but it can also be enjoyable. The relationship between my elder son and I is wonderful, yet he is still a teenager and there are many things that I just need to take a deep breath and slowly let go. Pick your battles and stick with those. Besides that, there is a lot of deep, slow breathing that goes on. If I picked a battle with everything he does that bugged me, we would have nothing but a miserable time.

A tame example:

I sat down to document some important information for an upcoming court appearance. I was stressed out of my mind and feeling like I was a goldfish when I talked, my mouth just opened and closed, opened and closed. Sometimes I didn't know if I was talking or just wanted something to eat. Maybe I am choking, or perhaps I am just a goldfish in a bowl excited for the falling flakes.

I asked my son to clean the kitchen, particularly the juicer that was covered in pulp. I went outside, onto my balcony for some fresh air and to take a break from my court documenting. As I was leaning against the railing, gazing into the field that surrounds the trailer, my son came outside and did exactly what I asked him to do, clean the juicer. My son proceeded to launch the pulp and gunk from the juicer over the deck railing and into the air, like scattering birds from a farmer's gunshot. Skins and pulp fell like debris from an airplane crash, scattered and strewn upon a wilted and sad-looking landscape. This landscape just so happens to be right beside my work and is my boss's property; as part of our agreement, I am to keep it tidy. Now, thanks to my son throwing the pulp over the railing, it is anything but tidy. Thanks son, I thought in my head, but what came out was, "What in Sam scratch are you doing?" (My mom always used to say that; I still don't know what it means). Very calmly, he turned his head in my general direction and replied like I was stupid and wasn't sure what just took place, "I am cleaning the juicer." Well, like being in a shower with no soap, I stood there confused about what to do. What else can I do but raise my hands in the air like saying, I don't know, shrug my shoulders and say,

"Of course." He goes to walk back inside and I look at him expecting him to say something else, something smart or funny...nope, he just goes back inside. He returns about fifteen seconds later as I stare at the mess, only to start bashing the top part of the juicer over the railing. I cannot help but stare like a bird watcher catching a glimpse of a rare species who is too in awe even to take a picture. He leaves a mountain of pulp along the railing and now on the deck. He proceeds to walk back inside when I again say, "What in Sam scratch are you doing!?" He replies, "Starting compost, it's good for the soil."

Inside, I wanted to soak up all of my angry red blood cells and shoot them out at him like paint balls, and hope at least one stung a bit. Then I would be low on my platelet count and I would still have pulp in the field to clean up. After all, it is a field and he did as I asked. Compromise, Clint, compromise; "Could you at least wipe off the railing?" I asked in astonishment. He calmly looked at me with a creepy, owl-type head turn, bent over to pick up a piece of cardboard off the deck floor and blasted the rest of the pulp off into my boss's field below my railing. Better yet, he threw the cardboard down right back where he found it, as I always taught him to put things back where you found them. Like nothing was wrong, he went back into the house satisfied that he was on the receiving end of a job well done.

Raising teenagers can be stressful on its own, without adding to the stress of another separation. Do not lose sight of your older child in the dust cloud, because when the dust settles, they will be nowhere to be found, on the inside at least.

25. Going Crazy

Stress affects your ability to act rationally

September '09

It is seven in the morning, the start of my work shift. The nurses and care aides meet at the nurse's station to go over the previous shift's reports. The nursing report starts and I hear, well, I don't hear anything right away; it is more what I feel.

I can feel my heart beating faster and faster. As it speeds up, I can feel the beating and pounding from the inside out and I can't stop it. I cannot control it and it refuses to go away. Like the beating of a battering ram against a fortified door, it continues on. The advantage the door has is weakness; it eventually will break and let in whatever is trying so ruthlessly to get inside. My heart feels like this, quickly and consistently, noticeable only when I am awake; but my chest won't cave like the door. I want to be like the door so I can feel the release, the end to the pounding. Whatever wants to come in or leave, I just wish it would. I wish for this to stop. Maybe what is coming in the door is not good, but how could it possibly be more convoluted than what exists here now? If I could just open it and let it out, feel the release, and stop the pounding, just for a minute! I suppose my heart is stronger than any door as it will allow for nothing to come in or out, it will not cave, and the pounding keeps going. The pounding of my heart is like a recipe, a pinch of this stress, a dash of that stress, two heaped tablespoons of, "what the #@$%." By themselves, they are clear and somewhat manageable. My thoughts and stress for my son are the ingredients, which on their own, can be dealt with one at a time. The problem arises when the stress piles up, new stress is added and eventually, like a recipe, you start the mixing. Once the ingredients are thoroughly mixed, like my thoughts, they blend into one, making it difficult to see what you started with. My centrifuge of emotions is nothing more than a blender leaving me with mixed thoughts and increased stress, now worrying when it will be over. What used to be minor stresses have combined with the major stresses and have all joined forces to become the super power controlling this acrimonious mind-set that

is becoming

my chaotic

norm.

"Good morning Clint," I hear, but that reminds me, I have to call my lawyer sometime this morning. I wonder what my lawyer wanted. I did not get a chance to return her call. I bet it's bad. A call from the lawyer is not usually good news. Damn his mother for doing this! Can she not see that he is only three years old and he needs both of us, not just her because SHE doesn't want to share him? Sure, I believe in "life after love" (Cher). It's a life of stress and misery. Then I remember, Halloween is coming and I have no money for a costume for my little guy. I cannot afford anything. WHY IS SHE DOING THIS? Speaking of affording, how am I going to afford my phone bill? They called and gave me my last notice. Crap! Oh well, so I will be without a phone, so what? I need my phone to call my lawyer. I should have been a lawyer. No, I couldn't handle dealing with people's petty crap all the time; on the other hand I would have tons of money. I forgot I need money for my car payment next Thursday. I need to pay that before anything else or I am in really big trouble, but I need to pay my phone, and for my son's hockey. What to do? I forgot about groceries, I needed to buy those. Cripes! "Clint!" I hear in the background. How am I going to get groceries with this cheque? I hate her! Hate isn't a nice word, fate rhymes with hate, and maybe this is my fate. No, bait rhymes with hate, maybe I am the bait, just the worm waiting for the end. "CLINT!" Again someone calls me. "Ya" I say, clearly dazed and not listening to them. "I asked you how Mrs. Anderson is coming along with her walking program setup by physiotherapy. You are her care aid aren't you?"

"Uh, ya. She's doing really well with it. I recommend we keep her on it."

"Are you ok Clint?" the nurse asks me.

"Oh yeah fine," I say, "Just something on my mind is all."

"How is your court thing going?" She asks, and I reply, "Ah you know, up and down, kinda like what got me into this mess." Everyone laughs.

I leave report and start getting my cart ready for the morning. "So how's it going?" my partner asks. I want to say that they are brainwashing my son to hate his daddy's house, my elder son is extremely upset by all of this and it is reflected in his recent drop in school grades. I just got an email from his teacher; can't she see what is happening?

My ex's lawyer doesn't even know me and she's fighting to keep my son from me. I hate her lawyer. No I don't, I don't hate. I can think what I want to; I think I hate her. I have to think positive. In a few years, this will be just a drop in the bucket. My bucket is overflowing. I want to shrink myself and grab a tiny little surfboard and catch a wave out of my bucket. On the other hand, I could just empty the bucket and throw up in it. Oh, I don't feel well; I wish this pounding would go away. I wish it was pounding in my head, and then I could take something for it. I suppose I could take something for this anxiety and the pounding inside but I don't want to start popping pills. This will be over soon. When is the hockey season going to be over? Cripes! My son's hockey is killing me this year. New pads, tournaments, he has no idea, and right before Christmas. Christmas! How am I going to pull that off this year? I could pay my lawyer, phone bill, take an advance for Christmas, and suffer through January. The car payment is due in December, groceries, more things to worry about.

"Clint, how are you?" my partner asks. I hear her in the distance, kind of like a dream where things are blended and not making much sense. "Uh, good, and how are you this morning?" I reply. "I would be better not starting at seven!" she says.

Seven was my favourite number as a child, I don't know why, it just was. I have a tribal tattoo from my shoulder to my wrist and wouldn't you know it, there is a distinct unplanned seven on it when I look in the mirror.

My older son is thirteen-years-old and was born in the sixth month; my second son is three years old and was born in the eighth month. Seven is in the middle, suggesting equality. The sixth month has four letters, the seventh neutral month is five letters, and my younger son's eighth month spelled out is five letters - they all equal thirteen. That is how old my elder son is. If you subtract the age difference between the boys, which is ten years, you get three, the age of my little guy. My elder son's name has six letters and my little guy's has seven, added is thirteen, subtract the age difference between the two and you get my little guy's age, which is three! My older is thirteen as I am writing this book, subtract seven and you get six, divide that by how many boys and it is three, the age of my little guy. My younger is a Leo, the Lion. Leo is three letters and Lion is four, add them together and it's seven! My elder son's sign is Cancer, the Crab, they add up to ten letters, the age difference between the boys, take away my little guy's age three and you get seven! According to Answers.com, the number seven is in the house of the Libra, Libra is the seventh sign. God rested on the seventh day and created the Sabbath, which also has seven letters. The number seven signifies balance. It makes sense, balance between my boys. Seven days in the week divided by my two boys is three and a half, equal time with my boys. Three and a half again multiplied goes back to seven. I am thirty as I write this book, subtract the age of my boys, which is sixteen and you, get fourteen, divided by two is SEVEN! Notice the year, 2009. Nine minus two is seven...creepy!

Maybe I don't work here as a care aid at all. Maybe I have lost it and am a resident here and my illness makes me think I work here. These aren't my friends or co-workers at all they are my caregivers. Imagine dealing with me every day, thinking I work there and trying to help other residents. Gasp! That is why I live in the trailer on work property; it is not a separate house but a special room for people like me. Gasp! No, if I had a mental illness I would not be able to acknowledge that I did, right? I don't know. (SLAP!) Get a hold of yourself man!

26. YOUR CHILD WILL SEEK OTHER ROLE MODELS

When the parents are busy fighting with each other, sometimes the kids are lucky enough (sarcasm intended) to have their mom or dad find a new partner, yet another person to join in on the fight between the parents. Someone who knows absolutely nothing aside from the one opinion told to them, which they quickly adopt as their point of view. Now things are getting cloudier by the day, the fight becomes all about the parents and is no longer about the child. They force the child into a shell. Like a snail, the child slowly wanders about, without direction; like the snail's shell, going round and round. As the shell continues to grow, it continues to spiral, going nowhere but round and round. Consumed by this shell, the children will want to find a way out of the convoluted mess. When they poke their head out of the shell, what will they see, or I should say, whom will they see? They will be looking for someone to help them out of the shell but who is it? Well, it is not the parents; they are nowhere to be found. They are hidden in the dust cloud that has yet to settle. They may see a clear image of an aunt or uncle, older sister, or perhaps a family friend. In my case, it was my uncle. He made me laugh and always made me feel good. Better yet, he made me feel important. He always seemed stress-free, and we just had a good time. As I got older, I admired him because I learned, in time, that he was like anyone else with bills, stress, and whatever else, but he never showed it. He didn't appear to let stress bother him and that reflected on the people he was around. Everyone laughed and felt good when they were around him.

Every child has a hero, and when they have to give their speech in front of their class, most often that hero is their parent. For others, like myself, this was not the case; my hero was my uncle. My uncle was the Lieutenant who saved this mere, weak soldier and turned him into a strong young man.

My point is this:

When there is stress and fighting, the attention strays from the children to the fight, and the child will seek someone who makes it better. You just better hope it is not an older child who gets them into drugs. Hopefully, like with me, it will be someone good for them, like a decent aunt or uncle, or family friend. Someone who will fill the void that you have created. When it happens, you will see that your anger has clouded your judgment, and you have lost the respect of your children. You may desperately try to get it back, but will it be too late?

DADDY SAID MOMMY UNMARRIED HIM. I ASKED MOMMY WHY SHE UNMARRIED DADDY AND SHE SAID IT WAS BECAUSE HE WAS STUPID.

27. RESPECT

Some parents believe that because they are the parents, their children should automatically respect and listen to them. Whether you think that this should be the case, or that times are changing, one thing remains solid. Children will remember everything their parents do.

Some parents may have a hard time with the idea that a fourteen year old, for instance, will argue with their parents, or not do something asked of them, like chores. These parents need to understand one thing. Children do not respect you if you don't respect them. How do I know this? I went to the source – my teenage son. Who better to ask than someone who is going through it?

Let's look at a typical example of this and brainstorm ways to stop this cycle.

My son's friend was fifteen and was constantly getting grounded. She was always doing something that got her into trouble. Not doing chores when asked, going out and lying about where she was. Her parents just blamed everything on the fact that she was a "troubled teen." For whatever reason, her mom made her feel bad all the time. Eventually, the chores kept increasing along with the punishments. For instance, if the bathroom wasn't clean enough she wasn't allowed to hang out with her friends because she had to do it all over again. The result was that she just started lying about going out, just to hang out with her friends. Her parents would catch this lie, a plea to be a normal kid, and now she was just a "lying troubled teen."

Think back to what transpired in my story: what happened when I reached the point of having absolutely zero respect for my parents?

She got into drugs. Now she was a "hopeless, lying, troubled teen with a drug problem". Now I don't know about you, but that's a fairly discouraging title to have hovering over your head, especially as a teenager. Try applying for a job with that name. "Hi, my name is Hopeless Lying Troubled Teen with a drug problem, and I would like to hand in a resume for the position you have available."

Name: Hopeless Lying Troubled Teen
1375 Dead End Road
Loserville
hopelesslyingtroubledteen@mail.com
Personal Profile: According to my parents, I am a lying, good for nothing, hopeless troubled teenager with a drug problem that will go nowhere in life and just hang around taking up space.
Education: Grade 10
Work Experience: None
Achievements: Under-achiever. I have not accomplished anything my parents would consider an achievement
Skills: Lying. sneaking out, taking up space

Her resume should have looked like this:

Name: Jane Doe
1375 Stevens Road
Kelowna, B.C.
janedoe@mail.com
Personal Profile: I am a person who is passionate about life, friends and family. I am a hard worker, and when given a task, I complete it to

the best of my ability. I am eager to learn new things and don't like to let others down. I am young, energetic, and respectful. I am also thoughtful, caring, and offer longevity to my employer.

Education: Grade 10

Work Experience: Cooking, dishwashing, housekeeping

Achievements: Voted most-likely to succeed by classmates; Trustworthy friend

Skills: Excellent communication skills, Able to work independently or in a group environment, Excellent organization skills

So let's do some brainstorming and see what her mother could have done differently:

She could have seen that her child had no respect for her and worked on getting that back.

She could have seen the lies and behaviour, as a hand stretched out, not a troubled teen.

She could have communicated with her daughter.

She could have understood that disciplining is okay when done without degrading the child.

She could have understood that her child's actions aren't just something that happened that day, they were the result of being made to feel bad for a long time.

No one likes to be disrespected – at home or at work. We all deserve the same amount of respect, even children. This mind-set will help break that cycle. It is difficult enough for adults to understand each other. It is even more difficult for adults to remember what it was like to be a kid, especially a kid who no one understands.

28. MY MAMA BEAR THEORY

How many bear attacks are from male bears? The majority of cases we hear about are of the mama bear protecting her cubs. If you think it's a good idea to go grab a bear cub, maybe take it home for a week, with the full intention of bringing it back to mama bear, you are probably mad, or you have lost your will to live.

Is it absurd to think that you can walk through the woods, find a mama bear with her cubs, and sit her down for a few minutes and say, "we should share this cub!" Yes, it's absurd. But consider this, if the bear saw you first from a distance, you may not be considered a threat. Your throat and major arteries would stay intact. As you get a little closer, you make sure not to make any sudden moves, and are very sure not to startle her. Then one day, the cub comes to you and you back off a bit. You most certainly do not grab the cub and hold it up in victory. Eventually, the cub's mother no longer considers you to be a threat. Now you are playing with the cub, swimming, having fun, and then returning the cub to mama bear. Eventually, mama bear allows these visits to go longer; maybe you take the cub for a few days, then four or five. Mama bear is comfortable with the cub's safety and her defenses have lowered. What seemed such an intense and possibly awful outcome has turned into time with the cub.

The most important part of this theory is that a human mother spends nine months growing and nurturing a baby inside her. She gets to bond with the baby in a way a man can only imagine, from every painstaking moment, from the nausea to the first kick, and, of course, delivering the baby. Just as a mother bear protects her cubs, a mother has every right to feel proud and protective over her young, all the while the father spends the nine months in his regular routine. This is a stereotype of course, as a lot of fathers try to bond with their unborn child by reading to them or rubbing the mother's belly.

So no matter what guys' feel, or girls feel, try to understand their point of view. Move slowly to make positive changes. If you haven't already figured out that males and females think differently, then this book is not what you should be starting with. If this is a "news flash" for you, then you may want to start with the book "Men Are From Mars, Women Are From Venus" by John Gray, then get back to this one.

29. My "A Dog Is A Man's Best Friend" Theory

I was born a man. Okay, maybe not a man—that would defy science and the Bible—I was born a baby, a male baby. Women might refer to males as these strange creatures who leave the toilet seat up; don't ask for directions; hurt themselves while trying to do manly things; and who revert back to their infancy when sick. Men might see things differently. For example, why waste all the energy putting the seat down when you're just going to have to lever it up again.

To understand this theory, you must read more into "Why A Man Thinks The Bathroom Is His To Control But Not To Clean" (I haven't written it yet). Whatever the case, men and women may not understand each other completely, and I think that's ok. We both need the other to complete things in our lives. That being said, a man will never know what it is like to be pregnant, grow a baby inside them, bond with them for nine months, and go through the painful experience of childbirth. Honestly, I am jealous (well except for the nine months and pain part), this is something that dads will never know and experience firsthand. What I do know is this, and I call it my "A Dog Is a Man's Best Friend" theory.

I cannot, rather we men cannot, give birth to a baby, let alone a dog. If you have tried, please don't email me about it, I don't want to know. The best we can do is to get a puppy and raise it. The puppy has been separated from its mother, and the man nurtures it, plays with it, toilet trains it, and gets people to watch it while they're at work or away. The dog and the owner develop a bond so strong, a trust so deep that the dog would do anything for its owner: guard the house, lay beside his when the owner is sick, run in front of a car to protect a child in their family. The owner will do anything for the dog: take it for walks, pay extraordinary amounts for veterinary care, for food, and even slip him the occasional burger at the drive-thru. Ultimately, the dog becomes man's best friend. The man did not give birth to the dog, heaven forbid, but has nurtured and cared for it, and in the process developed a love so strong that they are inseparable.

We are humans, and I think all of us, male or female, are born with the instinct to love and nurture. Females give birth; males do not, but the ability to love is within us all. By that I mean the natural compassion and drive to love and care for another, to raise a child and/or care for someone other than yourself. This seems to be an inevitable feeling for both men and women. If you are a couple who chose not have kids, or a couple who cannot have kids, chances are you have in your house either a dog or a cat, or maybe several. You may have a hamster, a goldfish, a hedgehog, or a bird. If you are single and do not want kids and do not have pets, you most likely want one or the other; or you enjoy your friend's cat, dog, niece, nephew, frog, lizard, or ant farm. Is this because we just love pets or because there is an unstoppable urge inside us to love and nurture? Maybe pets help us fulfill that need.

Could this be why we, as single people, meet someone, instantly fall in love, and then have it end in disaster, without giving a thought to time and progression?

Do we love less because we didn't give birth? Do we love less if we adopt? Absolutely not. I agree that females endure a great deal of emotion, love, and pain during childbirth. My point in this chapter is not to argue this fact, but to say that I genuinely empathize and cannot begin to understand or feel what they go through, or the closeness they must feel. That being said, I think it is also important to be mindful about what men go through during this process. Even though men do not go through this life-changing adventure, men do go through a life-changing adventure of love and nurturing of their own.

With all the changes, physically and emotionally that a woman experiences from conception to childbirth, they are ready to become a mother when the baby arrives. Instantly, things become different, the parenting instincts kick in, and the mother's life will be changed from then on. A father doesn't go through the same changes and must try to be a part of this process as best as he can. Fathers must make changes to get on the same page. Working late and coming home when supper is made and the kids are bathed and in bed will not win the love of your partner. Your partner, and new mom, needs you, as a father, to make some changes to be on the same page and work together. If fathers fail to see this and continue going for beers after work, working late, or continuing to do guy stuff on the weekends because it's "their time," the relationship will quickly fall apart.

A child will bring changes to a relationship, as a relationship between two people becomes a family. Parents must work together, see each other's side, and communicate any issues that arise so they can work them out together.

30. When the Alienating Parent Wants Back In

The alienating parent is now back. They say they have changed and now want to be a part of the child's life. They are sorry. They tell you about the counseling they took, they tell you they were wrong, and are so very sorry. Tears start flowing as they realize that they have missed so much time with their kids, and they are now pleading for access.

This is what I talk about when I say the parent who is doing what's right, not getting angry and doing what's best for your child, even though it goes unnoticed, really is a hero.

When this happened to me, my first thoughts were ones of anger. How dare they think that they can just come back into their child's life and expect to have ANY RIGHTS AT ALL? Then the flashbacks started. The noodles we ate in hard times, dropping my kids off at daycare, then going to work, and then picking them up from daycare. Some parents have two or more daycare centers or schools to pick their kids up from. The two jobs I worked to keep him in sports and dressed to the acceptable "coolness for school." Thoughts about my struggles went on and on, meanwhile, she was working, not giving me any money, and had none of these worries.

One of the good things about this, however, was the reward. The recognition of what a wonderful job I had done, being the bigger person all this time, finally presented itself. I didn't talk bad about my child's mother the whole time, and now that he's older, he knows who was there for him. He loves me, and I know it for certain. So what do we do as parents?

(This is a good time to do the exercise from chapter 9)

We really have to dig into our deepest love for our children and realize that the children will eventually ask about their missing parent. We have done what is right this whole time and we need to continue doing it. Even if, in your mind, they don't deserve to see the kids, the kids deserve that right. This will be a long process and remember, take baby steps. The absent parent (if the custodial parent agrees) has to understand that this isn't going to happen overnight. The children don't know you, they may be uncomfortable, and it will take time to establish trust. Start with a day here, a day there, and be glad that's all you're getting. Work slowly on increasing the time but do so with caution. If you don't plan on keeping this up, don't bother, you're just hurting your children more. This has the potential to affect your child and their future severely.

If you are the custodial parent, I suggest you immediately consult legal advice, child professionals, and have things strictly monitored. I would also personally ask for a letter from the parent's counselor they "said" they went to.

MY SON WAS IN THE TUB AND ASKED WHAT THE WHITE RINGS WERE AROUND THE TUB. I SAID, "HARD WATER." HE SPLASHED HIS HAND AND SAID, "NO, IT'S NOT HARD."

31. ASBESTOS

Asbestos was a popular mineral; a superior fire retardant, it was mined for its use in housing - mixed in concrete, wiring, and walls.

Slowly, the people who worked in the asbestos mines started developing severe lung diseases and cancer. It took years of research to pinpoint the problem. One study I read said that researchers did a fifteen-year study to monitor cancer in asbestos miners and others working with this product. Eventually it was labeled as "a deadly cancer causer" and removed from every house, and the people exposed to it were awarded compensation. Can you imagine something being so deadly, yet it took years for people to find and learn the truth?

Parent Alienation is the same. Right now, we are seeing how deadly it is, but research and arguments are still continuing. Children continue to suffer, and one day, it will be more recognized, be illegal, and be well known as a killer. Let's not wait fifteen years to do another study. It may be your child who dies before it is labeled as illegal and deadly.

32. You Can Walk a Mile in My Shoes or a Smile in Your Own Shoes

Before we went to court, we ended up agreeing on an eight and five day rotation, his mom having the eight days, myself five. I did it to stop the cycle.

More time with a child makes it harder for the alienating parent to emotionally abuse them, and gives the alienated parent more time to show their love and defuse the abuse. It gives the child time to see more from their point of view and realize that what is being taught to them is untrue. In the beginning, I reacted quickly and immediately let them know that this behaviour wouldn't be tolerated. I did so in the form of a letter and immediately sought out a lawyer. It changes things when the alienating parent knows that they are caught, but you still must be careful. Angering them can make things worse. Is it fair to have to compromise because you are worried that if you do not your child will suffer? No, not for me, but for my son, yes, it was the best thing for him at that time. His mom got her money from the government, plus she got what she wanted (to never have shared custody of our son, to be able to say that she is the primary parent). That was fine with me. A few extra bucks a month was worth my son's future. My older son also got some closure, after being an innocent bystander in the middle of an ugly war. He was told by his little brother that not only did he not want is brother reading him his usual bedtime story, but that he wasn't allowed to anyway. This devastated my elder son, and it showed in both his attitude and school grades.

Accusations of sexual abuse are very common in parent alienation. They are used simply as a tool by angry parents who are losing their battle to regain control; that being said, always be mindful of sexual abuse and if you suspect "real" abuse, report it immediately.

This was the actual letter my son wrote to his brother's mom. I ended up re-writing it and sending a slightly nicer one.

Dear 'anon'

I cannot believe what you
guys are doing to
I have been forced into
his same situation for
13 years of my life
and it is not what he
needs or wants, but the
things you have been telling
him and teaching
him are wrong and
cruel. Just because he
is three does not mean
you can choose what he
he likes he comes
here every 4 days and
says something different

(ex) When he had boys
problems i could not
say good night to him
even lay
in the same bed with
him at night, And for
atleast 2 months i could not
even read him a story without
kicking me or saying only
Daddy can sleep with me
you go, and all because
you told him that i couldn't
and for you to think what
you did about me is
totally obserd,

Another example this
weekend   We were
watching hockey and I asked
him if he wanted to play
hockey next year, he said
no I want to be a goalie
like you but in Soccer
not hockey mommy teach
me not to like hockey,
he came here every single
4 days and said i want
to play hockey i want
to watch hockey lets go
to your game, and like
i said just because
he is 3 years old
does not mean you can
tell him what he likes
and what he does not liked
and maybe he really likes
Hockey and wants to
be a great athletic
person and just because
you dont have a job
i am willing to get a
job and work my butt
off to help dad put
him Hockey cause i will
do everything and any
thing for him, and he
is my only bro and
you are NOT taking that
away from me!!!

119

Every situation is different, but these techniques, of reacting quickly and never giving up while being patient and loving, will win out eventually. My elder son's mother was quite the opposite. She was the one who eventually moved out of town, and I had full custody. Even though she was in another town, she would affect him just as much as when she was still in town. The lies about dad's house started and soon she was attempting to get him to choose to move in with her. He was eight! I stopped those visits simply because it was too hard on him. Children at a young age benefit from letting their parents make the decisions, whatever they are. They do not like being forced to make a choice and being pressured to pick a parent. They are frightened to hurt one parent or anger another. I immediately took my son to talk to a youth counselor who did a world of good for him. I don't know what they talked about when I was out of the room, but the counselor did explain to him that a decision of whose house he was going to live in wasn't his to make and he could stop feeling this pressure to choose. The judge would make the decision and he briefly explained the court process to him. It helped him see that it wasn't his fault, or his choice, and he didn't have to feel bad. When they get older, they can benefit from making their own choices by getting to know more about the situation, and what they feel is best for them.

As the alienated parent, you are doing the right thing by not saying bad things about the other parent, even if the child says them to you. I diffused a similar situation by reading my younger son a book. That simple task turned out to be the best thing I had ever done. When he told me that grandma and mom didn't like his brother, or me, and he didn't either, I read him a book called "47 Beavers On The Big, Blue Sea," by Phil Vischer. It was about working together and I explained to my son that I loved his mom and grandma, and that sometimes we get upset but we still need to work together like the beavers in the book. It did wonders for him. Every time he thought someone was angry, or saying bad things about someone else, he would say that we needed to work together like the beavers. Adults should try to do the same thing.

Another way of getting my older son to understand our situation, and be able to help his little brother understand the situation, was with a DVD. This DVD should be in every parent's house that have been through, or are about to go through, a separation. It is called "Welcome Back Pluto" and it is co-authored by Dr. Warshak, author of such well-known books as "Divorce Poison" and "The Custody Revolution." "Welcome Back Pluto" is a DVD designed to help parents and children understand and overcome Parent Alienation.

It took thirteen years with my elder son's mom for us finally to start getting along, for her finally to realize what she had done. One day, I asked her, over the phone, why she couldn't send me any money for help with our son. She hadn't paid me a cent in all the years that I had him; he was in hockey and played goalie, which was expensive to say the least. All with no help from his mom, but she would occasionally send him money. My son had told me that he had heard his mother say that she would never send any money. This angered me, only because I thought, after all this time, how can someone still be so angry as to not help his or her child out. Sending him a few bucks was nice but times were tight, what about helping out once in a while with groceries? I finally asked her directly and threatened to take her to court for the back payments for the last ten years, which was a bluff of course. I didn't care about the money. I just wanted to know what motivated her. She said that she had always been aware that she was the mom who left and it would always sadden her, even though she made that choice. Sending him money wasn't her way of getting back at me; it was because if I were to buy groceries with it, her son wouldn't know that his mom was at least still there, in some way, helping him out. If she sent him a little bit of money, and he bought nothing but candy with it, at least he would know it was from her. In her mind, he would still know that she was still thinking about him and doing things for him.

I thought to myself, either the biggest B.S. line I have ever heard, or it makes perfect sense. Why didn't she say that before? Miscommunication due to fighting I guess. Now, if she sends money and I buy groceries, I make a point to say, "Your mom bought these," or whatever else we might be buying for him. She is happy with that, I am happy with that, and our son knows that his mom is still thinking about him. What a perfect system, simple, but took thirteen long years to come up with. So if you're a paying parent, or a parent receiving money, make a point of telling your child where the groceries or their backpack came from.

Time was ticking on and she started to panic, as the boy she left was soon to become the man she never raised. She did what it took to get back into his life. Counseling was a huge part of it. Slowly, I allowed more visits and now they see each other on a regular basis, and both are very happy.

After thirteen years of chaos and stress, both of my boys are doing wonderfully. My little one is as happy as can be, my elder boy is the same, and on the honour roll at school. My relationship with both mothers is great; we can talk about the things that involve our son's best interests in a friendly way. I hope everyone can learn something from my story, so you don't have to walk a mile in my shoes; you can walk a smile in your own shoes.

I LOOKED AT MY DAD'S CHEQUE FROM HIS BOSS. HE MAKES LOTS OF MONEY AND TELLS MOM HE'S POOR. HE'S A LIAR. I CAN'T TELL HIM THOUGH, BECAUSE HE MIGHT NOT LIKE ME.

Sixteen year old girl

MIDDLE

33. FIX YOURSELF BEFORE YOU CAN EXPECT TO FIX OTHERS

Have you ever been on an airplane? If you have, you know all too well about the boring introduction by the flight attendant telling you what to do in case of an emergency. One thing you might remember is that they tell you that, when the oxygen masks drop, the parent should put their own on first. Absurd, you might think, but it is for no other reason than if the parent were to pass out from lack of oxygen, there would be no one to protect the child. So start taking care of you and quit making excuses. Then and only then, will your child get what they deserve from you. Go ahead and put on the oxygen mask and breathe deeply. Fix yourself first, then you will see the path to your child's best interest more clearly, and your children will thank you for it.

I was watching MythBusters, a show on Discovery Channel. They build things to either confirm or disprove common urban myths. On one episode, they built an ancient rapid firing bow and arrow shooter. They spent a lot of time building this contraption and the first day they went to test it, something broke. The next day, they had it fixed. Their excitement grew as they could now find the answer they were looking for. Unfortunately, it broke again, this time in a different area. This happened several times and near the end of the episode, even though you could plainly see that frustration was setting in, Jamie **Hyneman** said that sooner or later they were going to run out of things to go wrong, and then it would work great.

Try not to get too frustrated when life gives you lemons. It's not an ancient weapon you're trying to fix; it's yourself. Take on each new challenge with the most positive outlook and energy that you can and when another challenge comes along, tackle that problem or challenge with the same energy, as many times as necessary. The good news about continually fixing things is that eventually, you'll run out of things to fix. Then, finally, you'll be handed a map to that place called Perfect.

There are needs we must meet to survive and function properly. Starting with breathing and eating, down to self-esteem, and problem solving. This is Maslow's Hierarchy of Needs and the theory suggests that you cannot move on to the next one until the previous one is fulfilled.

So let's say that you don't exactly agree with this theory, but you must at least agree that before you can help fix someone else, you must fix yourself first. In these break-up situations, there is probably an abundance of things that could be better in your own life. I know with me, I was in debt, miserable, angry, stressed, not eating healthily, gaining weight, smoking more, and sinking deeper and deeper into my depression. If this sounds anything like you, perhaps this will help.

I made a speech in college a few years back, and it focused on how your stress needs to go down and happiness up. I made a list and I have followed it ever since.

I got everyone in the class to introduce themselves and tell everyone how their day was going and why (go ahead think about your day – good, bad, horrible, or great). There were all kinds of answers, mostly negative ones like, "bad because it was Monday," or "bad because I am broke," or, "I was late today," and so on and so on. When it came back to me, I was just getting over some serious eye problems. I said, "My name is Clint Williams and my day is great because I woke up this morning, was able to walk myself to the bathroom, and was able to see and hear my family, who I will never take for granted. I have my health and so does my family. My son is a beautiful boy, and here I am at school learning about an exciting new career." When we stop taking the most important things in our lives for granted, everything else seems like a bonus. It's hard to do at times, but it is not impossible. I would like you, the reader, to participate in this as well. You will only need a pen and a piece of paper.

I want you to make a list, a list of things that are causing you stress. When you're done, read it over a couple of times and then separate that list into two. One titled, "Things I Can Change" and the other, "Things I Cannot Change." An example of things you absolutely cannot change would be the price of gas. When you have completed both lists (if they are on the same page), cut the page in half and separate the lists. Take the list that has the things you cannot change, crumble it up and throw it away. There! You have already started making changes; doesn't it feel good?

Now to tackle the other list: Start with reading the list again and really think about how you can change things. Think about how you can start changing the cause of your problems. Is it financial? If you're deep in debt, there are options. If you cannot get a second job, then you may want to call a credit counseling number. I know a few people who have and it changed their world. If your problem is addiction, make the step and get some help; making one call will not hurt you. If you have been eating poorly out of financial trouble or just because you want to...stop it! There are a lot of healthy choices out there that are also cheap; Google some. The fried, greasy foods are driving your depression and mood down even more. You will be amazed at how good you will feel with some greens in your life, and some exercise.

Whatever is on your list can be changed. Now this is not to say that it will be quick and easy and won't take hard work. You will find, however, that the simple action of making the first step to changing will make you feel better inside. The change has started, what a feeling!

I don't know if your family vacations were at all like mine. I remember the stress of packing, everyone being grumpy, shoving stuff in the car like clowns in an Austin Mini, fighting over the seats by the window, my parents bickering at each other about anything and everything. Once we crammed ourselves into the car and started on the drive, it was like an invisible blanket of calm pulled up over us.

When you're finally on your way, the stress is left behind and there is a calm feeling, created from knowing that you have done all you can do. You also know that if anything pops up along the way you will deal with it as and when it arrives. This is the feeling you will get when you start making changes in your life. You will be comforted knowing that you took the first step to changing and now you are in the car waiting for things to fall into place.

I believe that we cannot make proper decisions for our children when our lives are a mess. Although, I will often say that it's no longer just about you, you have to remember that you still need time for yourself as well. Stop with the guilt. You need this time for you and your kids will be fine. They will benefit from a less stressed parent and they will also benefit from being around other kids and adults. So try doing nice things for yourself every once in a while. Trust me, I know, as a single parent, not many others will do it for you.

I'LL PROBABLY GROW UP AND GET MARRIED AND HAVE BABIES, AND THEN I'LL GET A DIVORCE. EVERYBODY DOES.

Ten year old boy

34. What Doesn't Kill You Makes You Stronger

We've all heard the saying, "What doesn't kill you makes you stronger," and it is possibly true. As hard as it is to accept a difficult time in our lives, we ultimately have no choice but to deal with that adversity whether in a positive or negative way.

Do I support the "what doesn't kill you makes you stronger" theory? In terms of personal growth, yes; the trick is to go through these hard times, not expecting ourselves to miraculously end up stronger. How we face challenges and adversity is up to us. If you stub your toe and shout "Ouch! That hurt" and do nothing else, you haven't learned a thing. If you think "Ouch! I stubbed my toe, it hurts" and after swearing, think: (1) why did I stub my toe? (2) was I in a rush? (3) was there something on the floor I was trying to avoid? If we try to find out how we can make it better, then yes, what doesn't kill you can make you stronger. If you take the pain and continue to grumble about it without trying to make it better, then no, it will not make you stronger; it will make you angrier. Move the object that you stubbed your toe on and simply be mindful of it to avoid stubbing it again, thus making you stronger. You can make a choice, go through the inevitable rainy days and grumble about them, or learn from them and realize that, without the rain, we wouldn't appreciate the sunshine.

So you made the world record for beating the eating-200-hotdogs record. You ate 350 but blew an intestine in the process. You get an operation and all is well. You continue shovelling wieners down your esophagus trying to beat your 350-hotdog record. Now you may argue that blowing your intestine didn't kill you so it must have made you stronger. Hmmm! It's only a matter of time before your problem blows again. Why not learn from your poor, bursting intestine when the previous record was 200. Perhaps all you needed to do to save your intestine was to eat one less.

Wieners are a bigger problem than you or I might think. Some take in as many wieners as they can handle, then more. Some serve wieners to contestants, ruthlessly over and over, with no regard for the consequences or protection of the contestants. One wiener often is enough, and even that can cause irritability on both ends. We need to learn from this and become not wiener stronger but wiener smarter. (Yes, that was a metaphor for having sex with everything and not thinking about the consequences).

We grow and become stronger by learning where we went wrong and taking the initiative to use what went wrong to change it, turning it into that "stronger" mind-set. Without that drive, without that first step, as hard as it may be, you will be stuck in the rut of getting beat up and frustrated rather than getting stronger. Getting stronger doesn't just happen.

35. Reducing Little Stresses Can Be Huge

When you start with reducing the number of little stresses in your life, it is easier to move on to the larger ones. Eventually, you will find that what you've been taught about stress is false. Our world has been built around stress; it is a billion dollar industry. Why wouldn't they want to keep us thinking stress is such a killer? Years ago, I had barely heard of stress and now there are such things as taking stress days off work, there are even commercials about stress and the drug companies are all over it. We are made to think stress is natural for this new, crazy, and busy world we live in. We're taught to believe we can just take a pill to make it better, but this is not true. These pills will have side effects, and you will most likely need another pill to combat the side effects of the first one and so on. Drug companies will continue to pump them out making billions of dollars, and we will continue to think this is normal for this crazy and busy world we live in.

One of my stresses in life is grocery shopping. Maybe it's not for some, but is definitely is for me. So I stopped doing it. Well, after losing thirty pounds due to a lack of eating and feeling badly for my kids, who were eating anything that could be thought of as edible (including our leather couches) I knew I had to do something and that something was to start shopping again. This time, I picked a different store and set aside plenty of time. It went a lot better than it used to. Before, shopping for groceries was incredibly stressful, which started as I was leaving work and continued right through 'til I made it home. I was anxious and agitated the whole time I was in the store and every little thing seemed to annoy me. Now, by changing stores and giving myself some more time to shop, I can get my shopping done and ease the amount of that stress in my life.

I can usually feel anxiety and tension all day at work, as I know there will be the dreaded grocery shop after work. I set out, already a bit grumpy, planning to go in, get the essentials and get out. It's never that easy. When I pull into the parking lot, I quickly find that it's packed. This is the price you pay to save a few bucks at these giant grocery stores. People are walking out of the store with their carts like a constant ant line. How do I even get through the first stop sign? Grumble. I've already lost five minutes of my time goal. When I finally make it to an aisle to turn down it's just as slow. I am agitated, as people don't push their carts along the sides, but on a slight angle across the whole aisle. So now I'm driving at almost an idle, getting honked at by the driver behind me. I speed up a bit only to get yelled at and fingered by the jackasses walking to their car on an angle in front of me. I'm ready to leave already, but breathe deeply and continue on, finally finding a parking spot. I get out of my vehicle and proceed to get a shopping cart; of course I've forgotten the dollar the cart requires. I reach into my pocket and pull out a handful of change. Not even one looney, just nickels, dimes and a quarter or two. I dread having to go all the way into the store to change it, to wait in the line-up and come back out. So I wait outside by the cart return and beg the exiting folks to trade me their cart for a handful of change. Some swear at me until finally I get a yes. Perfect, in I go. Now that I am in, it's just as frantic as outside. I come out at the end of an aisle and get blindsided by a shopper rushing like myself, except that they swear at me like it's my fault. Grumble. I pick up the pace as I really want to go home, and someone pushes their cart in front of mine coming out of the aisle. I grumble at them – I had the right of way. Now the challenge of fighting with the line-ups; Sheesh, I waited twenty minutes once only to find out the line-up was actually all the way down the aisle.

Finally I can leave, with me ready to pop like a balloon at its bursting point. I forgot where I parked because of all the stress in just trying to find a parking spot. So I walk on an angle down the parking aisle checking out both sides for my vehicle only to get honked at by an oncoming shopper looking to park. DOES HE NOT KNOW WHAT I'VE BEEN THROUGH? Then, as if it wasn't bad enough, someone asks me if they can give me a buck for my cart and me wanting to just go, says "sure." Well I get handed a handful of nickels and dimes and pennies and I think to myself, ARE YOU KIDDING ME? What do I need more change for? Grumble.

We create our own stress – our lives are our own. If we are not happy with something, we DO have the power to change it. We have the power and the right to decide our fate, our feelings, and who affects them. If we made a bad choice, we don't have to continue down that stressful path, which will only lead to more paths of stress. We all make mistakes, the trick is to learn from them and move on in a positive fashion. We CAN stop stress and we CAN get the control of our lives back.

After experiencing a stressful event in our life, once it is over and done, we can reflect on it with a different mind-set, a different angle, and perhaps even laugh about it. If we can laugh at it down the road, can't we do the same when we're in the middle of it? Stress doesn't have to control us anymore.

36. My Flat Tire

Making changes in our lives is only half the battle. If we don't fix the problem, it will follow us everywhere we go and be with us in everything we do. Take my flat tire story:

During one of my life's most stressful periods, a really bad day got worse when on my way home from the grocery store, I got a flat tire. The only money I had was some small change and my cell phone had been cut off. I had no choice but to try to make it home on the flat tire, hoping that it wouldn't damage the rim. I made it home, slowly, and unloaded my groceries, then ran a hot bath (yes, guys do that) and tried to escape from the stress of the evening.

I woke up in the morning and walked into work, thinking about my situation. All day I thought about how I was going to get my car going without any money. Then I had an idea; I'll just rotate my tires. So after work, I rotated my tires and headed off to pick up my son from daycare. I still had the same problem, but now it was the back left tire instead of my right front tire. I had to pull over, walk home, and call everyone I knew to try to get my boy home from daycare.

The next day, despite having tried it and knowing it wouldn't work, I rotated my tires again. Once again, I had to pull over and call a friend. We got my car home and I thought to myself, I don't understand, I had a problem, I made changes, but then another problem pops up in a different spot.

I hadn't fixed the problem; I had just changed its location. It continued to cycle round and round. I took the tire in to get fixed and wouldn't you know it, the problem went away.

If you think this would be incredibly stupid of me you would be correct, yet we all do it. So how do we fix the problem?

We start by understanding stress and where it comes from. In doing that, we can be better prepared to deal with it when it comes. In earlier chapters I talked about trauma, how it can be buried away and forgotten about but people still act in a certain way because of the trauma, all without knowing it. This was validated and made clear to me by "The Stress Doc." To learn about stress release and ways to avoid burnout, please do what I did and look into the works of Mark Gorkin, "The Stress Doc." He is a licensed clinical social worker and is also known as a Motivational Psychohumorist™. His knowledge, mixed with humour, not only keeps you awake but also helps you understand stress, the reasons for that stress, and what you can do about it.

For example:

Let's say you had a sister-in-law who you didn't get along with. You couldn't stand her and even the thought of her upsets you. Years later, you are in a new relationship and your former sister-in-law has long been forgotten about. Along with your new relationship comes a new job and you start working with someone who, in some way, reminds you of your former sister-in-law. Your new co-worker is nothing like her and is not doing anything to justify your feelings, but perhaps she looks like her or even chews gum like her. Whatever it is that reminds you of her, it makes you upset and one day you end up getting into a heated argument with this new co-worker. You dislike her and use the well-known phrase, "I don't know. There's just something about her." It is not about her at all! It is about you and what you went through, which you didn't deal with or release. It is about what you have tucked away that haunts you without you even knowing it.

Have you ever had the pleasure of witnessing someone snap over something small and petty, perhaps in a grocery store, at work, or in a bank line up? If you have, you would have noticed everybody around just looking at each other, shrugging their shoulders, maybe there was some snickering, some eye rolling, but everyone is mostly quiet, and in awe. Everybody is wondering what got into him or her. Maybe it was just a jar of pickles that was not priced correctly, or the bank teller asking them to wait just another minute. What got into them?

It wasn't just a single moment that made them snap, but many unresolved issues that have built up, and, with no more room for storage, hit a point of a forced release.

This forced release can be barking at someone, or can be even more severe like hurting someone. By the time this point is reached, do they still know what they are doing? Is it controllable or have they just temporarily lost their mind until that pressure is out, until the release ends?

Before it gets to this stage, understand that some stress in your life may be unavoidable and out of your control, but what is controllable is how you release that stress. Everything, when it is past its full capacity, will break – a balloon full of air, a dam with water, a bridge with weight, and us with stress. It is extremely important to be aware that we can prevent this from happening by constantly emptying our stress vaults. Ensuring that they never reach their full capacity and create a forced release. This can be done in a number of ways:

You can tell the person you're having problems with about what is causing you to feel at odds with them. This helps more than you might think because it helps people see how their actions affect others.

You can vent to a friend or family member.

You can write a letter, saying everything you want to say. Even if you end up throwing it out; it is still a great way to release stress.

I wrote my own letter, addressed directly to my stress and it was a doozy. It helped me a lot.

I was going to include it in this book, but it really needed some censoring so it could be published. It seems that after I censored it there wasn't much left, other than a few random letters. Instead, take this very moment to go get a pen and paper and write your own letter to stress. Trust me, it will make you feel good.

P.S. If you have to sensor as much of your letter as I did, it's probably best you throw it out anyway. The release is still achieved.

POOPED PARENTS,
PARENT POORLY
Unknown

37. YOUR BALLOON

Have you ever filled water balloons? People, like balloons, come in all shapes and sizes, some short and round, others long and skinny. What may be the bursting point or "forced release" for some balloons may not be the bursting point for others. Everyone reacts differently in a situation and some have a smaller capacity for stress than others.

A balloon can only take so much before it bursts. Some become huge in size; some burst right away. They each have their own individual level of tolerance and capacity. That's why it is extremely important to release frequently, until you find out which balloon you are. When you get used to it, you'll find your capacity, and then you'll know when to release the pressure well before you get to your breaking point – whatever that means for you. It is a constant process, and the more you are aware of this, the easier it will be for you to live your life happily. Some may call this your personal bubble. I call it your balloon. Once you get to know yours, you won't be afraid of the forced release or "pop." You will find that you start manipulating it yourself, like a clown making balloon animals. Trust them, tweak them; have fun with your balloon rather than fear the "pop."

38. Your Career and Your Happiness

Jobs can be the ultimate cause of stress. A person unhappy with their job is a person unhappy in life. If you are not happy in what you do almost every day, and find yourself spending more time with people at work than your own friends and family, you need to make a change. At least you need to explore other options or ways to make your job better.

I know change is difficult and scary, but it is always possible to change. Trust me, I know that finding a new job or going back to school is difficult with kids, especially with little or no support from friends or family. Make finding a career that you will be happier doing a goal, and research it; I tried tons of different jobs from construction to landscaping to graphic design and a whole lot in between. When the jobs didn't work out, I tried inventing things or thinking of commercial ideas. I still say that my one condom commercial idea would have been a Super Bowl Success.

I tried seemingly every job out there until I finally stumbled upon my career as a healthcare worker, which I absolutely love. I work with the elderly, and a ten-year-old child with Autism. I get to enjoy helping people at both ends of the spectrum. Making a difference in their lives is definitely something that I can fall asleep to at the end of the day. It wasn't out of luck that I found my dream job; I found it by throwing caution to the wind and trying new things.

My experiences:

I exhausted my construction dreams with my experience as a drywall taper. I was in my twenties and was so sure that, this time, I would stick with it and make it work. I called a friend of my brother-in-law and said I was ready to commit to him, work hard, and have a career. He said he wouldn't be making money off me for at least six months so I had better be sure, because if he was going to spend his time training me and it worked out, it would be worth it later. I assured him that I had thought long and hard about it and I was as serious as a zit on prom night, and he agreed to take me under his wing.

He gave me a pair of stilts to practice on over the weekend, as I would need them on Monday. I was a little afraid to put them on, as I am afraid of heights, really afraid of heights. I am afraid to be as tall as I am. I took them home and barely took them off all weekend. I was getting almost comfortable on them when Monday came around.

Day 1:

Monday morning arrived and we were at my first house, kind of scary. It was big and hollow-sounding as there was only drywall and mud everywhere. An odd and distinct smell lingered in the air. Hard to explain really, kind of a mix between wood, chemicals, and a bit of gas (and I don't mean the metered kind).

He took me down into the garage to get started with the "easy to learn stuff," and pushed a button on the stilts, which I, quite honestly, hadn't noticed over the weekend. Apparently, the stilts have settings. He pushed the button and elongated my stilts from my comfort zone on level one to LEVEL 9! Now I don't know if I am the only kid to catch an unplanned and unnecessary glimpse of his dad's penis and remember thinking...THIS THING GETS THAT BIG! Well there I was at twenty odd years later thinking...THOSE THINGS GET THAT BIG! I was shaking like my mom's top drawer as I strapped those giant stilts on.

Imagine standing on stilts high enough that you can just touch a ten-foot ceiling. You then add a lovely counterweight, which is a bucket of mud in one of your hands and a trowel in the other. With what hand am I supposed to wipe the unmanly tears of a schoolchild from my eyes?

Well, I don't know about you, but even on the flat ground in my shoes, my equilibrium gets thrown way out of kilter by simply looking straight up. Now somehow, in a euphoric state, I was supposed to keep looking up and start applying mud from my trowel hand that I dipped into the bucket in my other hand and fill a stupid hole with mud.

To add to my concerns were the encouraging words of my boss, "At this height if you fall, don't fall with your hands first, you'll break your wrists!" So I'm thinking, best-case scenario, I end up with a cracked cranium, possibly a punctured lung, all for the glorifying job of filling a hole with mud.

Maybe this job isn't for me, but I never give up on the first try because you never know. New experiences take a while to get used to and you have to give them an honest chance. Stick it out for at least a month, then make a decision, is my general rule.

Day 2: I quit.

Do you know what is less manly than walking over a plank over a twenty foot drop, 9 feet above the plank on stilts to look up and chuck mud in a hole? It is not only getting one foot out and sobbing like a school kid worrying how you are going to get back, but trying to do it on a now slippery surface as I just involuntarily urinated on the plank.

Ok, maybe I didn't urinate on the plank but what I did do was get light headed and knew what my parents meant by living in the 70's. The problem is when I get light headed I get nauseous, like on rides at the fair. C'mon now, I grew up with two sisters; it's a miracle I have any testosterone at all!

I did the only thing I could do and that was to brace myself against the wall, listening to my boss's encouraging words, "Chicken, Wussy, Girl! Just back up Sissy!" Well, once I finally managed to get down and onto flat ground, I decided that the job wasn't for me.

Of course, after that I tried many more jobs from landscaping to less muddy construction, without a single one tickling my fancy. I then started going through some common phases of job seekers. The first phase for most new job seekers is the "work hourly or commission." Despite the choice, when after the boss has filled you with so many ideas about the money you could make, you pick commission. Commission is just a glorified way of asking someone to sell eighteen hundred dollar vacuums to a person with little time left on this earth. Do you know what's worse than selling a vacuum to a ninety-year-old lady who tells you she doesn't even buy green bananas anymore? It's her son or grandson poppin' by for a visit while you're doing your demo in her living room. Here I am trying to sell this lovely, just under two thousand dollar, bargain; a vacuum that they can't lift, but acts as an air purifier and will extend their lives past the already ninety-eight-ish mark. Of course, they would have to purchase the overpriced vacuum with the inheritance money of the now red-faced angry son and/or grandson. This job just wasn't for me.

So I entered the next phase, which is, of course, the starting-your-own-business-before-you're-twenty stage. You can guess where that went. The next phase was inventing something, which I did, of course, and again you can guess where that went. Nowhere. Then I had the greatest idea ever! It was an idea for a commercial. I was sure it was so good that I had to make money on it. It was a condom commercial (Ok, stop laughing, I know, single dad with two kids by two moms writing a condom commercial). Anyway, I tried to market the idea and apparently companies have their own teams on payroll and do not accept outside offers. Ok, fine. But they are missing out on this:

A guy sitting at home, clearly bored out of his mind, gets in the car for a drive, just to get out of the house. He drives to a car dealership where there are tons of people and banners flying. He sees a banner that reads, "Free Hotdogs!" He quickly makes the turn into the dealership, excited as he just got a free lunch. He gets a hotdog and is trying not to look like he is just there for the free lunch; he starts walking around pretending to browse. A salesman walks up to him and asks him if he needs any help. Just as he was about to reply no, a voice comes from out of nowhere and says, "Yes, does this model come in red?" The man and the salesman look down to see that the hot dog is the one saying this! The salesman hesitantly says, "Yes, we have one in the back." "Great! We'll take it," the hotdog replies over the man's desperate attempts at saying no, he was just here to browse. The screen would then go black and the words would read:

If you let your wiener make the decisions, Use a _____ Condom!

Work experiences, taking a chance and seeing opportunities will create good things. Maybe at first your experiences will be negative, like getting a job that doesn't work out. You've gained experience and who knows, maybe five years later when you are struggling for credit or have a problem at customer service you'll run into someone you used to work with. My life has led me on such a path full of good friends who have helped me along the way. Friends like Gloria and Ed (whose real names I won't mention) who have helped me in ways that I just cannot believe. There are types of people who do good things for others, not because they want recognition but for the opposite. They do not want to be glorified for what they do, which makes them even more super. I won't mention their names either; I will just say they rhyme with Lon, Dorry and Aunt Betty.

My point:

My point is, whether you believe it spiritually or not, we are all designed differently, to do different things.

I tried numerous jobs because, well, we are here for a long time (regardless of the saying, "We're here for a good time not a long time"). Trust me, if you are not having a good time, life is a very long time.

How can you possibly decide what you want to do for a living after taking one course, or doing one job, and having nothing to compare it to? They say people change careers between three and five times throughout their lifetime. I tried them, gave them a chance, hated most, and learned from them, but they just weren't for me. That doesn't mean that those jobs won't work for someone else though. I have a friend in Sheet Metal, not for me but good for him. Many people have told me that they can't understand why I love what I do as a care-aide. They truly have no idea. What I do is help people do the everyday things that they can no longer do on their own. I assist them with getting that bit of dignity back in their lives. When I see a smile on their faces, mine is blessed with the same gift. I have found my meaningful job, helping others. Every day is different and enjoyable.

I once had a conversation about this topic with a man in his fifties, and he told me he didn't think it was possible to switch careers at his age. He had had his job since he was still in school and had climbed the ladder to the top. Even though he was making good money, it was making him miserable. But that job was all he knew, what was he going to switch to? I told him an inspiring story about a sunflower and said, "If I can find the motivation to finish my book and bring in positive change from a sunflower, anyone can see their own opportunities if they look for them and keep that door open." He said that there was one opening as a manager in a different area and I told him that was what I was talking about. "You're starting to at least think about it now, unlike before when you may have passed up numerous opportunities simply because you didn't see them." Another possibility is that you may like your job but dislike things about it. Perhaps it's the employees or maybe the management. There are always things you can do to better a situation.

If you're an employee and stressed out in your job, then I recommend you get your colleagues together and pitch in to buy your boss or yourself a book by Mark Gorkin "The Stress Doc." It is titled "Practice Safe Stress." He does a wonderful job at showing everyday workers the stress they are experiencing at work, and the different reasons for that stress.

Those reasons mean different things to different people. It may be that you believe you aren't being heard and all the good ideas that circulate among your colleagues don't go anywhere but in the garbage. Management may not be giving their hard workers and dedicated employees enough praise and respect, but rather they only interact in meetings about the things they are doing wrong. It may be you just don't get along with other employees. Whatever the stress that is affecting you at work, you are not alone. Stress affects everybody, including management who may or may not see the bigger picture. Eventually, the stress our co-workers and us experience gets the better of us and we, "snap, lose it, or have a breakdown." This stress-induced blowout isn't just related to work issues. By this point, things that you've hidden and think you've forgotten about start to come forward. Now, you are not just dealing with the immediate stress that made you snap, you are dealing with all the stress you haven't dealt with yet. All these triggers amplify this blowout into something a lot more catastrophic.

If you are happy in your career but feel like you're not contributing to society, or you think your job just isn't that important, think again. Everybody has a purpose, and everybody contributes to a cycle that has to involve everyone to continue on.

Let's take the idea that we are all equal, no one is better than the next person, regardless of education or personal drive that may be different than someone else's. Without each other, it just wouldn't work. Without each other we would have nothing. A doctor needs patients; a counselor needs people with problems, without them, they would be over-educated and unemployed. Pizza delivery people bring us food if we can't pick it up, allowing us to relax and have fun. Without each person needing something that someone else can fulfill, what would we have? We respect doctors, specialists, and the people who help us when we can't help ourselves, but where would they or anyone else be without people to help? The secretaries keep doctor's appointments flowing; mechanics fix their vehicles so they can get to work. When they go grocery shopping, the underpaid grocery clerks ring in their groceries so they have food to eat. Carpenters built the house they live in; the labourers hauled the wood, cleaned the site and dug ditches. Heating and cooling workers repair and maintain their furnaces, or air conditioners, while plumbers fix the toilets. A pool boy cleans and maintains the pool, and perhaps the yard as well. Those working in the coffee shops get people functioning in the mornings, and give them a smile that makes them smile, which is passed on to others; and daycare workers take care of our kids while we're at work.

Maybe without that smile: He was the one who was upset because his un-aroused wife hired a pool boy to gawk at, after he worked all the time and was never around. The doctor was agitated and distracted that morning as he went to pick up his coffee, missing the smile from the coffee girl, he wasn't focused and misdiagnosed a patient. That patient was perhaps upset about the news and didn't go in to work at the food bank. The food bank didn't meet their quota for that day, and children went hungry. The children didn't eat, and thus, didn't poop either. The lack of diaper consumption slows down, and diaper companies lay off millions of workers. Those workers try to find jobs but slowly lose their homes as well. The influx of unemployed people dramatically increases charity food banks and government funding. Cutbacks are made to accommodate this food funding and layoffs are made globally. The fire department takes huge layoffs and fires start burning out of control. The world quickly ends with hunger and a fiery inferno all because one coffee shop person didn't appreciate their job and didn't give out one smile.

Ok, maybe I got a little carried away there but you get my point.

If you're unhappy doing what you do, then change it. If you can't change it, change the way you approach it, or find opportunities to make it better. You don't have to do something monumental to help change the world; a happy, smiling face from someone passing you your morning coffee when you're feeling a little grumpy, may brighten your day and make you smile. You pass that smile on to someone else and it is passed on to others as they do the same. Who knows how many people were affected by that one smile, but it was a job well done. So don't kid yourself, you're more important than you might think.

39. The Moth at My Window

I live in a cozy, two bedroom home (what some would call a trailer, but I see as an elongated house) that someone, as a sick joke, attached, what appears to be, a trailer hitch to the front of it.

As a smoker, I frequently go outside onto my deck to get some fresh air. My deck is elongated and strictly single file. I don't have a light outside the door and it's quite dark at night, as I don't have a glass patio door. I leave the light on in the kitchen window, which is only a couple feet away from the door so I can have a bit of sight outside.

I watch a welcome friend, a moth at my window. He sees the light and wants in, perhaps for warmth, or perhaps because that's all he sees in this darkness and that is simply where he must go. He hits the window and dances about, up and down; side-to-side, fluttering in what seems to be a panic, to get in. He continues to be denied entry, yet continues to pursue his quest of getting inside, or, more accurately to the light. He knows enough to know that the light is there, and that he hasn't reached it, yet doesn't realize his plan isn't working. Other bugs, winged and wingless, see his countless attempts and marvel at his great idea. Before I know it, there are countless creatures flying around the window, some hitting it directly and trying again, some walking across it.

I left the light on and every time I went back out for "fresh air," there were even more bugs. None of them were by the door, all at the window where the light was. Throughout the evening as I came outside for a smoke, opening the door every time, there seemed to be more bugs, little ones, big ones, all flying in the same scattered, up-down-hit-the-window-and-try-again method. I see why people get bug zappers. They see or feel the warmth of the light, get zapped, and it's finally over. All thanks to the moth that started it all, and the rest followed.

I can appreciate that they may not have the brain capacity to think beyond their very simple thoughts; however, they are clever enough to start as a caterpillar, make a cocoon, and mature into a winged creature. Yet not once, with my door opening over and over, did any of them get the instinct to fly a couple feet over to the warm air and light coming from the open door.

Not one bug seemed to think, "Well, this isn't working, can't we have a bug huddle, like in football, and at least talk about this antenna-bruising plan that clearly isn't working?" Maybe flying through the door and getting swatted isn't such a good plan either; however, it opens the doors and windows to other options. As with our stress, when we get wound up and start something, we have to finish it, prove it, and with that we keep digging our hole deeper, even losing the original point. Even though we know it is not getting any better we are blinded, hitting that window time and time again, refusing to consider any other option. Sometimes we just need to let it go and walk away, even if only for a day, then come back with a new, and perhaps clearer, thought process.

My point is that we need to start thinking outside of the box, or in this case, inside the window. We must realize there are many answers and solutions, not just the ones we can think of offhand. Unlike the moth at my window, we need to take that important first step in looking for another solution. We can argue about differences such as parenting, religion, or things we are raised to believe are right. When will we see that arguing about it is getting us nowhere? We (people, parents, society) are deep inside our own little boxes and we fail to see any other point of view.

We don't have to agree with another's suggestion or idea, but we certainly need to understand clearly that what we are doing is as redundant as the moth hitting the window over and over. If you're in a rut, stop thinking like the moth and explore other options, opinions, and opportunities.

40. NEGATIVITY AT MY DOOR

As I went outside for fresh air one evening, grumbling about my life, it started to get a bit windy and I had to cup my hand over my cigarette to light it. With the wind picking up, I noticed that my moth friend had left. Perhaps conditions had finally gotten so bad that this stupid moth actually decided to leave. Then it hit me; here I am making fun of a stupid moth as I continue to do the same thing. I continue to go outside for a cigarette even though it's going to kill me one day, because I am stressed, I want to grumble about my life, and I never make any positive progress. Not only am I worse than the moth, I keep opening my door and letting the negative thoughts in, which keep me right where I am; smoking, stressed, and grumbling about my life.

Being negative is much easier than being positive. It's easy to be positive in the short term; like being happy because it is your day off tomorrow, or because you are doing something fun that night, but in the long-term it is difficult. This is because, not only does being positive require more energy, it is also difficult to believe in something you cannot see or feel. Negativity is easy. We can see our bills piling up, we can feel our anger toward our ex, or anyone for that matter, and it's quite clear to see that things just plain suck. Trying to remain positive long enough to see that it will bring positive things and deter negativity usually wears us out and we go back to inviting negativity in. The difficult part is to constantly believe that good things are coming, not see or feel the instant benefits, but still know that they are coming. We would rather see or feel instant feelings of negativity than future feelings of happiness.

As I stood there, with my cigarette, I pictured myself as a doorman at a fancy restaurant, only I'm not letting invited guests in. I leave the door open and welcome and greet negativity as it comes. As long as that door is open, they just keep coming, and as a greeter, I shake their hand and welcome them in. "Hello negativity, come on in. Glad you could come, Pain and Personal Anguish, it's been too long. Oh hey, Can't Pay My Bills and Hate My Life, plenty of room left. Well if it isn't The Knife in My Back, I haven't seen you in a long time, although I always felt that you were near."

When I realized what I was doing, it was too late. The place was filled with negativity, and there was a long line waiting to get in. I slammed the door and a few still snuck in, so I bolted the door. The inside now was filled with negativity but I opened another door, a positive one. Even though I had to clear out and deal with what was inside, at least no more were coming in and adding to it. Eventually, the same door I kicked them out of started bringing in Positive Knockers and I welcomed them in. I still get the occasional knock on my door from the other side, and some get in through the cracks in the door, but the room is now filled with positive guests, and it's easy to kick the negative ones out.

To achieve great things you must remain positive at all times and not let negative thoughts hinder your progress. Successful business people and millionaires all know that the way to success is to have your goals made up and forget that failure is an option or even a word. There is no such thing as failure only positive strides forward. They will tell you to think constantly about your goals. This could be achieved by putting up pictures of things you want, such as a house, a car, or an island in the tropics. The constant and positive reminder fuels your brain and you subconsciously will make decisions and seek people who will benefit you along your path to success.

41. The Power of Being Positive

I think the biggest problem with how we deal with stress these days is the popularity of negativity. It seems as though one has to be angry and upset to fit in, especially to get a point across. Why is this? Why can't we deal with the same stress but with a positive outlook? Well, we can. Just like many world-changing events, it will take time to create change, but with persistence, we can make it happen.

If you come to work late and you are super stressed out about it, slam your bag or briefcase on the desk, and start complaining about traffic and how stupid people are, usually your boss and co-workers back off, sympathize, tell you to relax, and that your day will get better. Try rolling into work with the same traffic situation, but whistling and cracking a joke about why you are late. All of a sudden, you're told that you don't take your job seriously and you're in the boss's office for an attitude adjustment and a lovely speech about dedication to the company.

Just because I refuse to join this group of negativity, and don't believe that I should complain about something just to demonstrate that I take it seriously, does not mean that I don't take it just as seriously as the next person does. Having this type of positive attitude, where you cross that bridge when you get to it and let things roll off your back, will unfortunately lead to the label of "someone who needs to mature and who should take their job more seriously." With me, people will be waiting a long time. I take everything just as, or more seriously, than most, but it is my delivery that keeps people laughing and reduces stress. People will eventually join your positive bubble and see that you can have fun and be responsible at the same time.

If you come to work whistling every day, happy, and positive, then people will assume you don't have any problems in life. Everyone has problems in their lives, and whether you complain about them, shrug them off, or fix them, it is no one's business.

I was at work when I overheard, "He's still young, he has no worries, he has his two boys, and cheap rent." Wow, I thought, that coming from a middle-aged woman who has her house paid for and her kids are grown up. I am a single parent of two boys, one full-time, one-half time who is an hour and a half away, meaning a three-hour round trip every pick up and drop off. My older son is in hockey, I am paying my lawyer more money than I am making, living in my boss's mice-infested trailer, on work property. It must be nice that I am young and have no worries; I haven't seen it myself though. I haven't taken a holiday in five years because I can't afford to. I constantly struggle with my bills and to keep the boys dressed and well fed. The difference, however, is that I don't come to work every day and complain about it. I talk about the things I enjoy, like my boys for example.

Mean or negative people are usually trying to cover their own sad situation. It makes them feel better to put people down because of their jealousy or insecurity. Take this negativity as a compliment, you must be doing something right to have people jealous enough that they feel compelled to try to bring you down. Negativity is a sign of weakness, happiness a sign of strength; the strength to endure whatever comes and remain positive. Negativity is the easy way out. Try being positive about everything for even one week. Don't get too ridiculous, but try it. You will see that it really is a challenge. Being negative and complaining about others, your bills, your life, and your job, is much easier than keeping a positive attitude that things will get better. There is the easy way and the challenging way. Which will you choose? Complaining, like popping a pimple, may relieve some pressure, but it doesn't fix the problem. Stay positive, laugh more, and don't get sucked into everybody's downward spiral, for negative people are simply people who have given up.

The reason I talk about relieving our stress is because, as much as we think we can ignore stress and be the cliché saying, "I do everything for my kids," remember, we must fix ourselves before we can expect to fix others. When we finally see how our stress is being passed onto our children and how they are being negatively affected, then and only then, can we truly care for our children with an open and stress-free mind.

FEAR LESS, HOPE MORE; EAT LESS, CHEW MORE; WHINE LESS, BREATHE MORE; TALK LESS; SAY MORE; LOVE MORE AND ALL GOOD THINGS WILL BE YOURS.
Swedish Proverb

42. It Wouldn't Kill You to Be Funnier

Have you ever picked your nose discretely and got a bigger chunk out than you expected, then panicked because you had nowhere to wipe it so you pretended to scratch your nose and stuff it back in? Gross, but seriously, ask a friend or even a random stranger this question when you're bored and just watch their reaction; it is funny.

I do weird things like this when I get bored, or just want to get a laugh, either from myself or from their reaction. People may think you're crazy, but it's fun and they will laugh (even if not until much later) and they will spread that laughter to others.

I have put together a starter pack, which you can use if you're feeling like you want to be weird and laugh sometime.

Clint's Tips on Funny Things to Do

When talking to someone (especially if they are nagging you for something), look at the outer corner of his or her eye. It doesn't matter which one, just look at the outer eye instead of directly at them. To them it looks creepy and unusual; they don't know where you are looking, only that something is off. The trick to pulling this off is to listen to what they are saying and fully engage in the conversation as if nothing is wrong without looking directly at them but not far away, otherwise it looks like you are ignoring them.

If you have a shovel handy and some hard soil, stick the shovel firmly in the ground and tuck the handle under your shirt when no one is looking. Lean forward so it looks as though you are on an impossible cartoon kind of lean. Be super excited and point somewhere in front of you and yell, "HEY LOOK AT THAT."

When people are crowding you in a line-up, turn around and say, "Hey! Can we find some other time to practice for the bobsled team?" This gets the point across and will spark a laugh or two.

Go into work and tell people about the dream you had about eating the world's largest marshmallow. When you woke up your pillow was gone, continue the joke by bringing a few feathers with you for effect and throw them in the air as you cough throughout the day.

Do funny things on April Fool's Day and expect a return prank. It's all in good fun.

The next time you make a bet, add in a "my crotch is itchy." This means that whoever loses the bet owes you one or as many as you bet on, and can be redeemed at any time. When commanded, wherever the loser is they must yell this out. It can be whatever you make up at the time of the bet, "my crotch is itchy, I just pooped" or whatever. I assure you this is funny.

Laughter helps relieve tension and stress, as well as anger and depression. Laughter releases endorphins, which are our body's natural painkillers. It also decreases stress and boosts the immune system. So don't think of laughter as being immature, laughter is quite the opposite; it is an imperative tool, which is crucial to our health and well-being.

43. I Don't Have a Button for That

Well, wouldn't you know it; the moth at my window didn't learn a thing. He didn't make another super fancy cocoon and turn into something more beautiful, or smarter, he just got a job.

I've suffered for many years from a condition called Ankylosing Spondylitis (AS). It's a chronic inflammation of muscles and joints that in time, causes the vertebrae of the back to fuse together leaving the person arched forward and in tremendous constant pain. After going from doctor to doctor, specialist to specialist, I realized that inevitably I was headed for a life of pills. The problem was that I don't like taking pills of any kind, so I looked for other options.

I joined forums and talked to an awful lot of people with this disease and others similar to it. Some of the feedback I got was to avoid red meat. Some said to avoid animal fat altogether. Animal fat is known as an inflammatory, meaning, if you have an existing condition such as AS, or Rheumatoid Arthritis (pain due to inflammation) an inflammatory agent on top of that just increases the inflammation, making it worse. I didn't know whom to believe, so I followed my old system. Try it for at least a month....

I decided to jump in with both feet and tried eliminating all animal fats from my diet. I quickly found out that doing that was more difficult than the disease I was dealing with.

I eat healthy and don't go to fast food places often, but, if I were in a pinch, I would go to one that had these great chicken wraps.

When I started cutting out meat and animal products from my diet, I stopped at the fast food place with a friend of mine. The majority had animal fat as an ingredient. After looking over the menu, I thought I'd just order the chicken wraps without the chicken. It would be a veggie wrap, I thought. That was until I tried to order it. "I'll have two chicken wraps without the chicken," I said to the voice on the big board. There was an awkward pause, followed by sounds of confusion. "Um...uh...well...uh...I'm sorry but the chicken wraps cannot be ordered without the chicken."

Puzzled I said, "Well can't you just not put the chicken in it? I'm not looking for a deal, I will pay the same price just don't put the chicken in it."

Again I heard, "um...well...uh," then what came next I could not have been prepared for. "I don't have a button for that."

Seriously! Are you kidding me? I know we're in the electronic age and all the tills have pre-set buttons for each meal, but seriously! Are you kidding me? I said to the fellah, "Okay, so how about you go ahead and push your little button, charge me for the chicken wraps like usual, but here's the clincher, just before you are about to put the chicken into the wrap, DON'T!"

"I'm sorry sir, I can't do that...I don't have a button for that," he replied.

Well, I know one thing, I had a button and he had just pushed it!

Getting mildly agitated by this point and the line-up backing up, I found myself raising my voice, not yelling, but I was frustrated. I took a deep breath and asked him again, "Push your $&%# button and don't put the chicken in it!" Well, this turned out to be a hopeless cause. Apparently, there was no button for this and the fine fellah just couldn't do it. I grumbled and just got a coffee. All this and not even a smile and have a good day.

Now I know why they say vegetarians are skinny. It's not the lack of eating meat; it's the lack of eating anything at all because there are NO BUTTONS FOR IT!

We don't have to be a button-pushing moth at a window. We can think outside the box...we don't need buttons; we need our common sense. We can do things outside of the narrow-minded thought pattern we get stuck in so often.

MY DAD LEFT BECAUSE I WANTED TO RIDE MY BIKE MY WAY AND I TOLD HIM TO GO AWAY. HE DID AND DIVORCED MY MOM.

44. CHANGE IS GOOD

An elderly man I once cared for told me that one of the health care workers who also helped him did everything wrong and it upset him. She said to him, "I am not doing anything wrong, I have been doing this for 18 years, I think I know what I am doing." His reply was "Did it ever occur to you that you have been doing it wrong for the last 18 years?"

If you haven't seen the movie "Groundhog Day," with Bill Murray, I highly recommend that you do. It's about a weatherman who is covering the "Groundhog Day" ceremony in Punxsutawney. Ironically, the ground hog's name is Phil, as is Bill Murray's character. He relives that day over and over, the exact same song on the radio, exact same people, exact same day, over and over. It is a very funny movie, and I like to quote it often. When I'm outside having a smoke, it's like clockwork. The same cars pull in; the same staff members get out, the same "Morning Denise, Morning Liz, Morning Clint." I joke and ask, "Have you ever seen the movie "Groundhog Day?"

Some people dislike change while others fear it. Both, I think, find themselves going a little crazy. Change is good, even when we don't yet know it.

Now don't go all crazy, dump your partner, and fly to Mexico. I am simply saying that we are at work for a lot of our time, with the same people. We come home, do the same things, and wonder why we are getting depressed. Knowing exactly what your days are going to be like, day after day, leaves no room for imagination or anticipation.

Now granted, if you have kids, your options are limited. Do not think, however, that you can't make little changes that will benefit you. You can:

Rearrange your house furniture. This can help as it gives you a different, fresh view of the place you are used to.

Write down a list of things that you might want to make for dinner that are different; you could also do this for movies to watch, and places to go to. Put them in a bowl and pick one out every day.

If you are in a relationship, do the same thing. Let each other write down the things you both want to do. Pick one out every day. This could be anything from a meal idea, or a night out, or a vacation.

My son and I did this, and we, of course, have our funny ones. I picked out one of his papers and we ran up the road two houses and back the other way two houses, wearing only towels and singing his song; then when we got back, we made pizza. As weird as it was, it was fun and it was different. The next day at work, instead of knowing that I was going home to make something for supper as usual, I didn't know what I would be cooking, and it was nice. Even though they weren't major changes, they did make life more interesting.

I've made another equation:

(One day of routine) x (numerous days of that same routine) x (not letting your frustrations out) = A forced release.

If you look at weight loss or muscle building strategies, you will find that even our muscles need change to be able to develop over their current size or tone. Your diet requires change and certain amounts of nutrients to keep you staying fit and shedding fat. That's why many programs allow you to have "cheat days" where you can eat anything you want. This is good for you. Why? Once your body gets used to a reduced-calorie diet, it drops its calorie level as "your normal." So after a few weeks of seeing results, your body adjusts to your new calorie intake and makes that your new normal level. So in order to keep losing weight, you have to drop your calorie intake again – you see where this is going. If you kept reducing your intake to accommodate your body seeing this as your normal level, you will eventually decrease until you are eating nothing, and you will die. When your body gets to the two to three week stage of its new calorie level, you need to change it up, confuse your body a bit. You do this by eating over your new calorie level. That's why you're allowed ice cream or burgers on a diet plan. It sets your calorie level, once again, up to where it was before. Now you can do those two weeks again with the same results, over and over, as long as you keep changing what your body is used to. Your calorie level stays the same but your body keeps burning fat.

This process also must be taken in baby steps. Don't be fooled by television shows or record weight loss rumours. To do this process right, it takes time. A new lifestyle takes commitment. Everyone gets carried away and takes on too much when dieting. It is a huge change and must be done slowly. That change is usually what deters people from following it. Here is Clint's weight loss/health plan.

Start with a goal, either amount of pounds lost, or cardio time.

Break that down by the month, by the week, then by the day.

Deal with that day when it comes; don't worry about the month, focus on your end goal.

Know that doing something is better than doing nothing. Don't be fooled by thinking that you have to run for thirty minutes to start burning fat and seeing results. When I was short on time, I still ran for ten to fifteen minutes and I still saw huge results.

Restrict your calories a little to get results. Don't starve yourself. If you're going to snack, eat veggies; they are low in calories and chewing them burns the calories they might add.

Know that what will satisfy your hunger is the nutrients that your body needs, not a huge plate full in your stomach. You shouldn't ever feel "stuffed." We get used to a "full belly" feeling as being full, yet we still might feel unwell. This is because it isn't about being "full," it's about the nutrients that you put into it that your body needs.

Eating salads with mixed greens and things like, kale, spinach, Swiss chard, etc. give us important nutrients, so incorporate them into your diet. Once your body gets used to feeling satisfied without that "full belly" feeling, you will find that you will feel better.

Eat in moderation. We are told that we need so many servings of veggies, fruit, meat, dairy, etc. and we get overwhelmed. How could we possibly eat this much? Do yourself a favour and visit the Canadian Food Guide website. You will find that the suggested servings are tiny, and are all we need. For example, one serving of meat is about 4x4 inches, once a day. What do we eat? A full rack of ribs, or a whole T-bone steak with prawns for dinner. At lunch, we probably had a meat sandwich, and maybe for breakfast we had some bacon, and a sausage or two. The guide suggests that we need so many servings of greens per day and we think, how could we possibly eat all of that? One serving of vegetables is about a cup; in leafy greens that means a child's handful in one meal. Dairy could be as little as just one glass of milk. You should be able to fit your meal onto a dessert plate. This is what our bodies require. Anything over that is what we want to eat, not what we need to eat, and is causing us to be overweight. Keep your portions in check, exercise everyday if you can, and don't get discouraged.

Changes can be made most effective by being positive and visualizing your progress. Arnold Schwarzenegger's "Encyclopedia of Bodybuilding" first taught this to me years ago. He said to not just workout, but to visualize your muscle cells changing and growing with every repetition. I have practiced this since I was fifteen years old with great results. Some people have argued that I just have one of those body types that respond quickly to exercise. I, however, know my body and when I work out just to get it done with my mind elsewhere, I don't see the results that I get when I completely focus my mind. When I run, I picture the muscle tissue getting ripped and rebuilding, getting stronger.

Years later, this didn't sound all that crazy as I watched numerous shows, which revealed that there have been many studies showing that our brain can't actually tell what's real and what is not. If we stimulate our brain by thinking our cells are rebuilding, can our cells actually do that? Yes! It makes sense that if a guy can just think about sex, and not be anywhere near an attractive source and still get an erection. What forces that blood flow to the penis without any attractive real life person around? Same goes for women, don't kid yourself. If we can think about something that isn't near us and get aroused, the same must be true about other things, such as weight loss and muscle building.

I HATE MY SOFA. IT'S WHERE MY PARENTS TOLD ME THEY WERE GETTING A DIVORCE. I'LL NEVER SIT ON IT AGAIN.

45. Brent's Story

My friend called me out of the blue one evening. He opened up to me about his concerns that something wasn't quite right with him. Lately, he had been angry and snapping at his girlfriend, and his crew at work. This is very uncharacteristic of him as he practices positivity, shutting the negativity door, so to speak. Now he was finding himself letting the negativity in by the boatloads and he didn't know why. He went to the doctor and she suggested an anti-anxiety pill. He wasn't so sure, having never experienced anxiety but he knew he didn't want to take pills; he just wanted it fixed. He instead took some homeopathic pills and when they didn't help, he ruled out anxiety.

As our conversation went on, he started talking about his life and I just listened. What I discovered was that his girlfriend of five years likes to unwind after work with television, while he, on the other hand, doesn't want to come home every day just to make supper, watch TV, and go to bed, only to do it all over the next day. He used to enjoy going out, just to get out of the house. I said to him, "I think we have just found your answer to what's wrong my friend. Life is getting mundane, every day the same. How do you look forward to tomorrow, when tomorrow will be the same as every other day?" I suggested he talk with her and express this, as she was also experiencing his obvious attitude problem.

They talked and because she didn't want to go out every day, they compromised. A couple times a week they go out, maybe to a pub, a play, a movie, or whatever. This makes them appreciate the time they spend at home, when they make popcorn and watch the shows they both enjoy.

Let's think about what could have happened if they hadn't communicated what they were feeling. Your partner can't always read your mind and, without expressing your feelings, it will lead to destruction. He would have continued to hate his days and she would watch TV. Slowly there would have been no communication of "how was your day?" as both don't really care anymore. Why would you want to share your day with someone who doesn't pay attention to you or doesn't seem to care?

From there, the negativity door remains open and they become moths at the window, unable to think outside their boxes. Now there are feelings of anger and jealousy and, when there are children involved, an environment for HAP and PA has just been created.

A survey of a hundred people, half women, half men, revealed that the majority of partners blame lack of communication as the ultimate cause of their break-ups. The remaining ten per cent said they rushed into a relationship and found that they didn't have strong feelings for their partner but felt stuck. If you're in the majority of the non-communicators, start thinking about your partner and talk often. If you don't, someone will come along who does care, and by then it will be too late.

I WAS VERY MAD AT MY FATHER AND I WANTED HIM TO DIE SO I COULD REMEMBER HIM THE WAY HE WAS BEFORE HE LEFT US, NOT WHAT HE HAD TURNED INTO.
Nine year old boy

46. NOTELLY RIVER

If you have never been to the Notelly River, I will give you the directions but I am sure you will find getting there just as frustrating as I did.

To find Notelly River, head on down Notelly Road, this will seem like an eternity. Eventually, you will see a sign that says NOTELLY BRIDGE AHEAD. It is time to cross the bridge now that you've gotten to it. Just up the road you will get to an intersection, the signs will be labeled clearly, but the directions are a bit foggy. You will see a sign that says NOTELLY RIVER, and an arrow; you will also see a sign that says FIGURE IT OUT BY YOURSELF WITH NO POSSIBLE CHANCE, and an arrow. You, of course, will take the arrow pointing to Notelly River, but when you get to the sign that says YOU ARE HERE, you will notice that there is nothing there. In frustration, you try the other route, the Figure It Out By Yourself route and find that this is just as frustrating. You may get lost at this point and try to find your way back. You will take a left at the sign that says NEVER MIND, and proceed down the road labelled, FRUSTRATION AND RELATIONSHIP DOOM.

Do not confuse Notelly River and the Nottely River in The United States. Notelly River is difficult to find if no one tells you. No Telly = No Knowy.

If you don't tell your partner what is bothering you, it will build up. By not telling, you assume the other will know, should know, or will figure it out for themselves. Men and women are different, we all know this by now, and the only way to start understanding each other is by telling the other what is bothering you. Communication is the most important thing in a relationship, and still is, even when separated. Do not try to find Notelly River, try to find Talktoya Lake.

47. The Sunflower

Have you ever bought something, maybe a vehicle, or perhaps a pair of pants or a shirt, only to start noticing that you now see them everywhere? Instantly, it seems that everyone has seen what you bought and want to be like you so badly that they are rushing out to buy the same things! Unfortunately, unless you're famous, people don't care what you're wearing or driving (I am speaking for myself here, I don't know about you). We simply didn't notice them before, who cares about all the cars on the road, or what other people wear. These things just floated by us without a thought, and it wasn't until we had them ourselves that we became aware of them everywhere.

The same goes for positive changes and opportunities. If we are unaware of these opportunities, which float by us every day, they will just keep floating by. There are positive changes we can make and opportunities to grab a hold of every day, when we can see them. A random sunflower might give you hope and motivation, but it is different for everyone. So, in the event that you decide to make some positive changes, start with seeing the opportunities that float by you every day. Once you plant that thought you will become more aware of your surroundings. Go somewhere you wouldn't normally go to if you were invited, keep your ear out for job opportunities, they may start with a seminar or through someone you meet at a conference. Who knows, it could even be via a friend of someone you met at one of those things.

Whether you believe in God and Creationism, or in Evolution, both sides need to know one thing. The inspiration, hope, and positive drive we need to keep us going, is all around us. We just need to look a little closer, find what it means to us, and, most importantly, believe in it. Believe and let it help you succeed.

I live in a trailer with pine trees all around us; the pine needles cushion your step throughout most of the yard. I once saw spots of grass poking through the needles and thought it would be a perfect spot to plant grass, so my younger son could have a nice play area. I started raking, what turned out to be piles and piles of needles, down to the soil and grass that already existed, wilted, long and droopy. Some neighbours nearby told me that I would never grow grass there; the trees meant that there was too much shade, and too many pine needles. I carried on, raking and raking. My neighbour came over after a while and asked what I was doing. I explained to him that I wanted to grow some grass for my little guy to play in, although it sounded like it probably wouldn't grow well. He told me to look at his lawn, which was always as green as it could be. His landscape was the same as mine and he had just planted a bit of grass seed and watered. He gave me some grass seed and even spread it around for me. So I did as he said, I watered and watered, and wouldn't you know it, by the summer the doubters were commenting on my green play area.

It was too late to plant the small garden I wanted for the boys. However, my younger son was still so excited to plant the garden, that I did it for him in July, for fun. Again, skepticism rolled in about us not being able to grow anything because it was too late in the year. That is, until my neighbour's wife came by. She told me that I would still be able to grow some things, as long as I watered a lot. Well, that's just what I did, and our garden started growing in just a couple of weeks. Little shoots were coming up, and my son was excited, even if it was probably too late to eat anything from it.

The garden flourished, and by the end of August and early September, we were enjoying fresh lettuce, dill, kale, peas, and radishes. The beets didn't make it, but we enjoyed the beet tops in soups and salads.

The one thing I didn't plant was flowers, or more specifically, sunflowers. However, in September, I noticed a plant growing taller in the garden and wasn't sure what it was, but my first thought was, it is a sunflower. I thought it was strange, as I hadn't planted any. I called my neighbour over to have a look-see before I yanked it out, and she confirmed that it definitely was a sunflower. I asked her if she thought it would have enough time to flower. She was optimistic, but time would tell.

October rolled in, and the nights were occasionally getting into the negatives temperatures. The mornings were jacket weather for sure, and the sunflower was still there, budding, and so close to flowering.

October 23rd was the first time I noticed a flower blooming. It was kind of a nerdy, but exciting day. The flower wasn't facing the house, but through my kitchen window I could just see some bright yellow colour poking about. I went down to the garden to have a closer look. It wasn't fully opened yet, but if I had to guess, it was about halfway. I thought to myself, this must mean something, a flower I didn't plant, is just flowering now on October 23rd when the weather had been cold and frosty, and the rest of the garden was dead, dying, or wilted. Curious natured, and an obvious over thinker, I looked up the spiritual and botanical meanings of the sunflower and the answers I found were: A sign of warmth (like the sun), guidance, love, prayer: victory and longevity.

In such a time of stress and hopelessness for me, I thought what an inspiration that was. Victory and longevity – this was a sign for me to keep going. A little more over thinking revealed that the flower wasn't pointed at my house or me; it was pointed at the dead, dying, and wilted garden.

Then it hit me, in the cold, late October, one plant stood tall. It looked over the ravaged garden, and shone its beauty of sun, hope, warmth, longevity, and victory as the sunflower knows that next year's garden will thrive again. Do not give up.

Such as my life was at the time, a dying and wilted garden, I was inspired, uplifted and motivated by this sign. I pushed through the negative comments and worked hard on my book.

There are a lot of things that we don't see at first which we can use for inspiration, motivation, and positive growth. It may be a sunflower, or it may be opportunities floating by that we aren't seeing. When you can start to see these opportunities, whatever they are, embrace them and use them to get yourself to where you want to be in life.

48. STEVE

I always wanted a Rottweiler for a dog. A big ol' rotti in my yard, one who was just like my friend's rotti. That dog was great with kids and family but reeked of "GET OUT OF MY YARD," to strangers. My friend decided to breed their "purebred papered Rottweiler" and I reserved the biggest male out of the litter. We had all kinds of crazy names for what was to be this giant protector of the house.

The anticipation of our pup being born was torture for my son. A three-month wait seemed like a lifetime for him. I, too, was excited for this new addition to the family – one that was big and intimidating.

I got a phone call from my friend when the puppies were born. She said there was good news and bad news. I told her to hit me with it. She said that the puppies weren't exactly purebred, but that they were cute, and they had reserved us the biggest male. My son was so excited, how could I say no? "How not purebred are they exactly?" I asked. She danced around the subject, and a few weeks later, they dropped off our new puppy. He looked like a cotton ball that was dipped in chocolate milk and had gone through the dryer coming out super fuzzy, with little legs poking out the bottom. Well, so much for the crazy names we had picked out. He became Steve.

Steve wasn't the big ol' scary Rottweiler that I always wanted. As Steve got bigger, he got fuzzier. Instead, what I had was quite the opposite of a sleek-looking guard dog. What I had was a sheepdog with a drooling problem, who couldn't even grasp the game of fetch. He would get the stick and bounce around with his bum in the air, front paws on the ground, get ready to pounce again, waiting for you to chase him. Not exactly what I had in mind when I saw other dog owners lounging in the sun, throwing a ball for their dog, waiting for them to bring it back. Nope, fetch with Steve was quite exhausting, no lounging for me.

Steve is afraid of small animals, like hamsters, mice and cats; just seeing them, makes him run into the house. We have to brush him and trim him constantly, and even so, he's still so hairy he brings in everything from outside – pine needles, sticks, bugs, and when he shakes himself off, the floor looks as if we're camping outside. He's not a licker, but he does lick your kneecaps, and it's annoying. He drinks too much water all at once and pukes on the floor every time. He scares himself with his own tail if it touches him when he doesn't expect it. A weed touched him once when he walked over it, and it flicked back and hit him in the butt. He ran away so fast, and then tried to pretend like he was tough, turning around a half-acre away and barking. But we love Steve and we wouldn't trade him for anything.

My point is: Don't be afraid to try the things you think you may not enjoy – food, job, an outing - whatever it may be. You might just find some of the best things in your life weren't planned or even wanted.

49. My Son's Lucky Necklace

My son wanted to start playing hockey, but he was already nine-years-old and couldn't even skate yet. He hadn't stepped out on the ice at all, not once, so was unsure of how well he would play. He doubted he could catch up to the rest of the kids who had been playing for four years and skating for at least six.

I put him in every skating class I could find, including figure skating. The next year, I registered him in our local hockey league. He did great, though not as well as the other goalie on the team, but that was to be expected, as he had a five-year head start on my son. Tournament time came and he didn't want to let his team down, as he was still unsure of his abilities to play goal in a tournament. The coach had him play every second game, like usual, to help build his experience and confidence. The team did really well in the tournament and my son was quite pleased with himself, gaining confidence by the game.

The next hockey season was even better and confidence was seeping out of every bead of his sweat. He won an early tournament game against the toughest team, and after the game, without him knowing, I grabbed the puck. I carved a smaller round shape out of the puck, drilled a hole in it and gave it to him as a necklace. I told him that it was a lucky necklace and his winning streak continued. That was until they lost a game miserably – the final score was 7 to 1.

After the game, he threw his necklace at me and said, "So much for the lucky necklace." Later I explained to him that "luck" or success, is what we believe it will be; what we believe we can accomplish, and to have faith in that. It didn't matter if it was a piece of the winning puck I carved out, or just a rock that I gave to him. Whatever it is that we find motivation from, it will work if we believe it will. "So you believe in magic?" he asked me, like I was stupid.

"Well yes, I guess I do, because when you believe in being positive, magical things will happen." I replied.

"What about me losing?" he asked.

I replied, "You automatically look at losing as failure, and fail to see that losing and making mistakes is how we learn and get better at things. These things don't just come naturally to everybody. Your lucky necklace did its job perfectly well by making you lose that game because it is lucky to see what you did wrong because it will make you better; you simply failed to learn from it. Why did you lose that game, what did you do differently, were your teammates playing a different position than normal? If you don't learn from that loss, it will happen again. Knowing that and going through that makes you lucky.

Update:

My son doesn't play hockey anymore but when he did, he played with all he had. Even though he started late, he caught right up. He continues to do well from the life lesson that he learned from his hockey experiences. He is not afraid to make a mistake, or fail at something. He isn't afraid of trying something new and not being the best at it, or getting laughed at. He is not afraid of these things because, to him, he is learning, getting better, and moving ahead.

The most beautiful people we have known are those who have known defeat, known suffering, known struggle, known loss, and have found their way out of the depths. These persons have an appreciation, sensitivity, and an understanding of life that fills them with compassion, gentleness, and a deep loving concern. Beautiful people do not just happen.

Elisabeth Kübler-Ross, M.D.

50. The Fridge

After the separation between my younger son's mother and myself, money was tight and I was now looking at having to pay even more rent, and by myself. Life was discouraging, to say the least. I happened to see an ad at my work for a three-bedroom basement suite for rent. $600 per month, utilities included and I thought to myself, this had to be too good to be true. It was indeed too good to be true. Only the living room and first bedroom were carpeted. The flooring in the kitchen was linoleum (which was old and stained with a lovely color of what I can only describe as urine that blended well with the Robin Egg Blue), an apartment-sized fridge and stove. The rest of the flooring in the house was concrete, with what appeared to be remnants of a horrible orange paint job. It was now chipped and flaked everywhere, and topped with a lovely dressing of only the largest spider carcasses you have ever seen. Did I mention I hate spiders?

I had to make a choice. It was affordable, but absolutely, hideously disgusting. Before I made the decision, I thought of the only thing a manly man, trying to support his family, would think to ask himself. With my hand across my face, with my thumb on one side and the rest of my fingers on the other side, tapping my finger in the classic deep in thought look, I thought, what would Debbie Travis do?

I took the place and looked forward to fixing it up, until I started the first job of chipping boogers off a wall, then having to putty the holes left

179

behind, which brought me back to my drywall taping days and I cried like a three year old lost at the mall.

My elder son and I continued in our quest, and after a month or so the place looked really nice. A few months later, I came across an impossible deal for a stainless steel fridge that had been on my wish list for years. It was an Amana, stainless steel, with a pullout bottom mount freezer. Imagine that, our hard work finally had been rewarded in some way at least, Now we had this monstrosity of a stainless steel centerpiece that took up most of the tiny kitchen and only would be approved in a house with some rationale under the roof. Fortunately for us, I was single, and there was no such thing in The Guy House, The Man Pad, The Ken Den, The Testosterone Tower, The Bicep Bungalow, The Man Can.

We had many names for our place, my boy and I. We stared at the beautiful masterpiece every day, graciously polishing the exterior, and then we noticed something strange. No, not our reflection in the polished exterior, but that the fridge was keeping fruits and vegetables for extraordinary amounts of time. We once threw out some fruit that still looked good but we doubted it could keep fresh for so long. Fresh produce and a stainless steel man fridge, nothing could stop me now. This fridge was amazing and wonderful, so wonderful that the saying, "If it seems too good to be true it probably is" eventually cropped up. The basement suite only had a shower, no bathtub, and my little guy, who was two at the time, was taking his baths in the sink, as he didn't care for the shower. He was now too big for the sink, and with no other options available, we had to move to a place with a tub. No problem, I will just take the fridge, I thought. That was until I swapped places with a girl I worked with, and moved to an even smaller three, but really a two, bedroom trailer. So now, I just downgraded. I was thirty years old, renting a trailer from my boss, and living just off the parking lot at work. I always thought thirty would be different, you know, with a house, food, that kind of stuff. There was no room for the fridge in the trailer, but that was ok, honestly. The trade for a tub for my little guy was well worth it, and I would have done it again without a second thought. At least the fridge in the trailer looked somewhat new, not like the Robin Egg Blue apartment-sized fridge and stove in the last place.

We loaded the fridge and filled the freezer, and by that I mean we put the ketchup and mustard from the old fridge into the new one. There was, however, a big ol' box of waffles that we had to stuff in the freezer. That turned out to be a bonus. At that time, between paydays, most of what we had to eat was in the freezer.

Of course wouldn't you know it, I go into the freezer one morning and grab a bag of floppy soggy waffles, story of my life. I found myself muttering my famous phrase, "Are ya kiddin' me?" I felt the other food in the freezer and it was starting to thaw as well. Oh great, I thought, perfect timing and just what I needed! I left it in hopes that it was a defrost thing or, like most guys, thought that if I ignored it, it would fix itself. I banged on the vents in the back of the freezer. Wouldn't you know it in a day or two the fridge was back to normal.Maybe a good ol' Fonzarelli was all it needed.

The next week, I went to grab some milk for cereal for the boys and the milk was bad. This was puzzling because I had just bought it a couple days before. At this point, I was furious. I had to do something.

I hesitated to go to the maintenance guy, "Vally" because once before, in our old house, my old fridge quit when I blew one of the breakers. I had checked the breaker panel and the switches looked fine. I didn't know what to do, so my son and I, at 6:30 in the morning, muscled the fridge across the house into the living room where the outlet worked. Great, now I had a huge stainless steel masterpiece in my living room. Huffing and puffing, I begged Vally to come over and check it because there was obviously something wrong as I had checked the breaker and ruled that out. After grumbling and telling me, "It is the breaker" and me continuing to argue, he went over to my house to have a look. He returned about a minute later and said, in his almost Arnold Schwarzenegger kind of voice, "Put your fridge back, it was the breaker!" I was grinning and feeling a little stupid, and told him, "Thanks Vally, I love you." He grumbled something, as he walked away, not sure, probably that he loved me too.

This time was different, there was definitely something wrong with this fridge, no freezer defrosts like this and leaves the fridge warm too. It must be something in the cooling mechanism, I was sure of it. I grumbled as I started to toss food in a garbage bag, muttering bad things under my breath, blaming Vally for the lack of maintenance of the fridge in a rental suite. I was going to give him a piece of my mind, as I couldn't afford to waste groceries.

Well, it was a good thing that I did not go and start tearing Vally up about the fridge because as I was frantically and furiously tossing food out into a garbage bag some numbers appeared in my mind. I kept tossing, and then thought to myself, numbers? Hmm, numbers. I look up and wouldn't you know it, there was the dial for the fridge. Did I mention my little guy is good with numbers? He was so good that while getting his own juice from the fridge, for which I was very proud of him, he turned the dial to ZERO!

It makes sense now though, the first time this happened with the fridge my little guy was here, it went back to cool when he went back to his mom's. In a few days when I picked him up again, it went warm again. It's a good thing I am a quick learner and mechanically inclined, who knows how long this could have gone on.

The point of the story is this:

When your life seems at its worst and you don't know what to do, maybe your problems can be fixed with a simple solution (look for the dial, look for the dial!). Didn't we learn that back in school with the "KISS" theory? Keep It Simple Stupid. Try looking for the less complicated answers and stop expecting everything to be complex.

The answers to most of our problems are relatively simple, we just over think them, and look for what must be a complicated answer.

51. Think In Moderation

Thinking can be a good thing; however, you can get carried away. Always use caution when you're thinking. You don't even see it coming; you start thinking a little, around friends, about the situation you are in. Next you find yourself doing things like thinking when you first wake up, hiding your thoughts from others, and thinking alone.

Thinking should be used in moderation. You have to know how to handle your thinking and take precautions to keep you, and others, safe. Especially if you are thinking and planning to drive, you can call a friend or family member, or just stay at home and think.

Over thinking can lead to a confusion of thoughts. What once may have been a simple answer has been left behind because of over thinking. You think and think, then someone hands you another thought, just a quick one, c'mon. Eventually, you pass out. Your brain is done, given up, and declared finished for the day. Your brain can't handle any more thoughts and what have become new thoughts, are convoluted and far from helpful in this frame of mind. It has strayed so far from the simple solution that could have been. You wake up the next morning a little foggy, but you finally realize how unrealistic your thoughts were.

This cycle can and will be repeated, unless you go back to your first thought, realizing that thinking too much isn't the answer. The answer will be found by tackling the problem with a clear and rational mind.

IF I GO LIVE WITH
GRANDMA, CAN YOU
AND DAD STAY
MARRIED?

Seven year old girl

52. BABY STEPS

R eleasing the mama bear's claws takes time, so if you're the parent pushing for shared time, slow down and realize that this is a process.

For example: your personal trainer expected you to run five kilometres and lose thirty pounds in one month. That would be absurd to most of us. However, you start slowly running five minutes nonstop, then ten, thirteen and so on. Eventually, you're running your five kilometres nonstop, losing weight and reaching your goal, but it took time.

The mama bear realizes that slowly changing will get you seeing both sides. If you're the pusher, realize that pushing for court just costs money. You both can accomplish this without spending your down payment. Take it slow, gradually increasing with time, while working together, discussing what you didn't like about the arrangement and what you did. Compare and compromise, eventually things will please both sides but you have to be willing to be flexible. Do a month or two at a time, then re-assess, and make changes if you need to.

Any change takes time and dedication, whether it involves kids, jobs, quitting smoking, exercise, eating habits, etc. If we fail to see that we need to make these small changes to see the bigger ones, we will continually fail to reach our goal.

Every situation is different, and sometimes they escalate horribly and your child is stuck in the middle of an unfortunate, to say the least, situation. This book is about trying to make changes and it starts with small ones. So what can we do to try to change what is happening? Well, like in any war, I doubt both leaders will say, "Ok, that's enough. Let's call a truce." One has to be the stronger leader, laying down their weapons, and approaching the war with the idea of change for the good, no matter how hard it is. How do we do this? Well, we can look at trying some different approaches to everyday situations, and try to deal with anger in a different way.

Happiness and positive responses throw negative people off balance. Have you ever had someone raging at you, and your response is a smile and something like, "Wow, that vein in your forehead really pops up and turns a shade of purple when you yell." It may upset them more, but usually they feel silly and won't know what to say. Or perhaps they will just stomp away.

Contrary to what some may believe, anger is a sign of weakness, happiness is a sign of strength. Your child, after a while, will recognize how you keep the house stress free and things positively rolling. Children are better than we think they are at detecting stress.

Let's say your ex is dropping your child off at your house. Once inside and the ex has left, your child says something like, "I don't like coming back here, your house is always messy, and Dad/Mom says it's always like that." Before you start bubbling with anger, and say something like, "Well maybe they should get off their lazy butts and come do it," or "get their floozy to do it." Breathe deeply and understand that this is a great time not to be negative toward the other parent, no matter how difficult this may be. As hard as it is to say something nice to someone you wished would get an extreme chronic case of diarrhea and eventually die of dehydration, you might find that initiating, for the sake of your child, something nice and non-threatening may lower the fight/defenses of the other. Maybe not; however, it is worth the initial effort. Once the guard is lowered, only then can sense and reason be negotiated, so try a different method. Something like, "Well, Mommy/Daddy gets busy sometimes, but we always clean up our messes, right?"

This, first of all, gives a non-threatening and positive outlook on the negative comment to your child, as well as supporting an important life lesson. That lesson is of course that parents, as well as children, make messes but what's important is that we clean up after ourselves. It's okay to play with Play-Doh, as long as we clean it up after.

When the next pick-up or drop-off takes place, you can say, while grinding your teeth in the least obvious manner, something like, "Suzie commented on how messy my house is and that you say it is always like that. I stopped for a minute and realized how busy I have let myself get these days. I just wanted to thank you because I've been able to make a mental note to slow down" (just an example, as long as it is not threatening or abrasive). Whatever you say, don't say it in a cheeky way or it's just the same as a negative response. This being said in a genuine tone could be the first step toward defenses being lowered.

If you think I'm crazy, perhaps you're right, but I will remind you that this book is written from living with this situation, with my own two kids, for thirteen years of hell and experimentation. It might not happen right away, but you may notice that, the next time your child gets dropped off, there is no negativity. Whatever method of positivity you choose, remember the most important rule: THIS DOES NOT GO THROUGH YOUR CHILD. It should never be a message for the child to pass on. The child stays out of it, left unaffected by conversations that are only to be held between parents while the child is off playing, like they should be.

DAD COULDN'T REALLY BE AS BAD AS MOM SAYS HE IS.

Nine year old girl

53. PROGRESSIVE, MOMENTARY AND LONGEVITY ACTION PLAN

We are all patient when we are enjoying transitions in babies. First they are born; they lie on the blanket and eventually they make a huge effort to roll over. Are we mad that they can't roll over right away? Of course not, we are just proud. They then do a half roll and the hands go up in the air, like an almost-goal...but back again. They finally roll over, and when they do, it's a huge day. All family and friends are called. Next, comes crawling. They wiggle; they "schooch," and soon we're at the same anticipation level as when they rolled over. Do we expect them to crawl right after they roll? Of course not, it takes time, and in that time, we don't worry about how long it took to roll, we now look ahead with proud anticipation as they make their next step.

Now they are crawling, and we think about how we had it good when they weren't able to. Now we're picking everything up and frantically making sure the crawl-path is clear of danger. They start grabbing on to things and trying to stand. Again, as parents we encourage this, and on to the next step of walking. We're not always thinking about how long it took them to crawl; instead, we're thinking, they're almost walking. It's a new step and you are so proud. They take a step and fall down. Do we get upset that they fell? No, we applaud it and keep encouraging them.

Eventually, your baby is walking, and again, you call every family member and friend. You are as proud as proud can be; except, of course, now you are frantically clearing the walk-path, as well as the knee height path. So if we can all appreciate and applaud a baby's small step, how come we forget these steps in our own lives?

Is it because the word "baby" is in front of it? (Well, personally I think it's appropriate for the way adults act sometimes.) Where did this very encouragement and constant positive reinforcement go?

Most things fail because people want to see the result, rather than the path to get there. It is a long, hard road, and even though we teach our kids this, as adults, we can't be bothered. We are here for instant gratification. The result is that the end goal remains clear in our minds, and it excites us from time to time, but because we lack the drive to start, the drive to take these baby steps, we prevent ourselves from reaching our goal.

We can apply this to anything in life. We start with our own personal goal, small, but with the end in mind. Put pictures up and write yourself motivational notes. Know that the first step is rolling. It may be you want to get in shape, and you hear that running or cardio for thirty minutes a day is best, so you make that your goal.

If you think you will get up early, plug in your headphones, stretch and run non-stop for thirty minutes you will be more than discouraged (from my own experience anyway). I kept the thirty minutes as my goal, and how long I could run nonstop for, on any given day, were my baby steps.

I got out ready, ripping and roaring, just me and my dog Steve. I quickly found out that he wasn't the best running partner. In any case, when I was out of breath, it seemed like I had been running forever. I thought to myself that I must be at least halfway! I looked at my watch - exactly two-and-a-half minutes. I was panting, choking, and ready to pass out on the side of the road thinking, great, now I have to walk back. It may have only been half a block away, but when you're out of breath and with a large dog, it might as well have been a million miles away!

To add insult to injury not only did I have to walk back with a "not-so-attractive-to-women-look" of my panting, grunting, gasping for just a breath of air, but I also had to do it with a bag of dog-poo (thanks Steve). Well, let me tell you, this is no way to pick up girls! I mean really, what's my line going to be if I saw a cute girl running her dog and I have Steve rubbing his bum along the ground, a bag of dog poo in my hand, and myself trying to talk but making only noises like, gasp, pant, choke, gag, fart, cough, with one hand on a tree bracing myself. Not the time or the place to say, "So, do you want to do this same time tomorrow?"

In the end, I started running around a pond close to my house. That way, if I were to pass out, I was close enough to roll home later when I came to. I kept track of my progress and stayed out for the full thirty minutes, whether I ran or walked. So the first day around the pond, I did one-and-a-half laps. It might not have been great, but who cares that I can only do one-and-a-half laps before collapsing. I still walked, and ran, for the full thirty minutes. My goal was to increase the amount of time of continuous running, not increase the thirty minutes. Whether I ran, walked, picked up dog-poo, or passed out, it didn't matter.

By the end of the first week, and let me tell you that first week was horrible, I hurt and was too sleepy to get up in the morning, but after that, I felt great! I was up to almost five laps around the pond non-stop, and seeing my improvement gave more motivation than anything else did. I did it by pushing myself! Why did it seem so hard? I guess because it's easier to push someone else, appreciate and see his or her progress, than your own.

As we are grown-ups, and we don't like being referred to as babies, let's call it something other than Baby Steps, how about a Progressive, Momentary and Longevity Action Plan.

Any change takes times and dedication, whether it is kids, jobs, quitting smoking, exercise, eating habits, etc. If we fail to see that we need to make these small changes to see the big ones, we will continually fail to reach our goal.

Be a little more positive. When life gets you down and gives you lemons, you can make more than just lemonade.

I WOULDN'T MISS MY DAD SO MUCH IF I DIDN'T HEAR MY MOM CRYING SO HARD EVERY NIGHT. IT'S NOT FAIR MY DAD ISN'T HERE TO DO HIS JOB.

12 year old boy

54. WHEN LIFE GIVES YOU LEMONS

Y ou can actually do a lot of things when life gives you lemons. I have compiled a list for you to put on your fridge:

You can juice the lemon, take the seeds, and shoot the seeds at people. This is always funny and a great stress reliever. Simply place the seed between your index finger and thumb, apply pressure and shoot. Caution: always wear eye protection when shooting lemon seeds.

After juicing, paint half of a lemon peel with black craft paint. When dry, apply red dots; add a pipe cleaner for feelers or antennas, and you, and your kids, have just made a ladybug.

Make a lemon meringue pie.

Add fibre to any dish simply by adding lemon zest.

Make fish taste even better.

Make lemon pepper wings.

Carve out the insides of the bigger lemons and make helmets for the smaller ones.

Drink water with freshly squeezed lemon juice to help detoxify your liver and add Vitamin C to your diet.

Help protect against cancer and arthritis.

Make lemonade, of course.

Hollow out a lemon and stick it on top of a plunger that's been cut in half. Stick the plunger on your dashboard and have your very own lemon bobble head.

Stick a couple on your bumper with a sign that reads, Life gave me lemons and I'm taking them for a drive, what are you doing with your lemons?

55. Nutrition and Its Importance

One of the Ways I Helped Fix Myself

The first step you want to make is to add some greens into your life. The things that you may never buy at the grocery store are, in fact, the things that could be helping your mood or depression. If you don't need to improve your mood, greens will, amongst a ton of other things, give you the "B" vitamins your body needs for proper brain function; as well as other nutrients, which our bodies need to feel great and function properly. Other than a salad here and there, how many greens do we actually eat in a day, a week or a month? I talked to someone who didn't know what kale was. To be honest, two years ago I didn't either. Greens such as kale, spinach, Swiss chard, and arugula were pretty much unknown to my family other than the salad we would occasionally make with the traditional lettuce.

Kale and Swiss chard are a super source of vitamins C, E, and K, carotenes, chlorophyll, and fibre. They contain minerals such as potassium, magnesium, iron, and manganese, as well as vitamin B6, protein, calcium, thiamine, selenium, zinc, niacin, and folic acid. After eating these foods, you'll find your energy levels increasing, skin problems clearing up, and your mood will be affected positively.

I won't bore you any more with nutrient values, but seriously, take a look at these types of foods. Adding even a little of them to your life will help your health considerably. Try buying things you didn't before, things like beets, chickpeas, lentils, beans, pineapple, nuts, I could go on for a while here, and yes it does get overwhelming. If you are overwhelmed, resist the urge to revert to doing nothing. My advice is this: if you do anything in the form of nutritional change visit www.rawfamily.com. Now I don't receive any kickbacks from them, nor do I currently follow a raw diet, but they really helped change my life nutritionally. You will learn how to make smoothies, which contain things like fruits and greens. I know that might not sound great, people cringe even when I make them and tell them what's in my smoothie. Yet, smoothies are a great quick way to help get this kind of nutrition into us and our kids. They taste like a fruit smoothie and I have learned many tricks along the way. To my morning blend, I add fresh (and sometimes frozen) blueberries, banana, strawberries, and alternate between spinach, kale, and Swiss chard, as well as other leafy greens. It is a great way to get all the benefits of the fruits and greens we don't get enough of in our normal diet. Once you've made a few of them, you will start to experiment like I have. I add flax or olive oil for the omegas, or a little avocado, chia seeds, sprouts, fresh real lemon juice, no sugar added grape juice, or real no sugar added cranberry, or pomegranate - the choices are endless. Mine always taste fruity - I don't like drinking green juice, but people's tastes are different and according to www.rawfamily.com once you get used to the fruitier smoothie your body will start to crave a less-sweet one. This is an easy way to start a nutritional change and I highly recommend it. If there is one thing that deters people from new routines, it's inconvenience. Whipping up a smoothie only takes a few minutes and you can even put the fruit and greens in your blender the night before (just don't blend); add juice or water in the morning, blend, and it is done. My thirteen-year-old son loves them, as well as my three-year-old, so at least try it.

56. IF THERE'S ONE MEMORABLE THING

Whether it is in a relationship, a line-up, or ordering a coffee; in my experience, with everything I talk about in this book, the most important thing I've learned is this:

Empathy

Truly feeling, or trying to feel, what someone else may be feeling. Someone could have a headache and we think "that sucks," then carry on. Someone may be sad, angry, or just plain emotional. We may try to comfort them but we don't really know how they're feeling.

It was mastering the art of empathy that enabled me to do what I love for a living. A health care provider, like me, may never know what is really going on in the brain of a child with Autism, or what elderly people with Alzheimer's disease or Dementia truly experience. What I can do is to try my best and put myself in their shoes and try to understand, even just for a little bit, what they may be feeling and experiencing.

My understanding of empathy first started while trying to really see my ex's perspective. Why were they so angry, and doing and saying such awful things when I had done nothing wrong? That was my first mistake, thinking, without a doubt, that I had not done anything wrong. Obviously, at this point in a break-up, there is not much communication so how can we know how our former partners really feel? How can we know for sure that they didn't feel the same way about you as you did them? Perhaps you didn't love them, but they were madly in love with you, perhaps it was the other way around. If you were the one who was dumped, it would certainly be different from being the one who dumped. Perhaps it's just a matter of a wasted journey down a long road to get to this nowhere point that angers you, or them. It could be many things. We all feel and react differently to circumstances. Most times, it's with anger and we fail to see the other side, or we just don't care.

It is a very difficult thing to do, truly feel for someone who is making you angry, or may be sick, sad or in pain when you are not. It's always easier to give advice when you're on the other side, but what about truly feeling what someone else is going through? We can tell our friends that it will be ok, but we are not in the same place, mentally, and emotionally speaking. It's comforting, but what does that really mean to them, or to us?

When things get complicated, such as with a relationship break-up, usually it's a case of everyone for himself or herself. "They hurt me, I will hurt them, and they did this, so I will do that." We get clouded in our thinking, and see nothing but hate and jealousy.

We've already gone over the exercise in chapter 9. Let's do it again, but instead of blurring out your ex and yourself, blur out your child. What you should have now is a clear image of you on the left and your ex on the right. Instead of thinking about all the bad things, put the weapons away, the boxing gloves aside, and picture yourself in their shoes; thinking about you. If you can't come up with anything as to why they are acting the way they are, and you did nothing wrong, take a break, think about it, and come back to this exercise later. Eventually you will see that you are not always the perfect one, and neither are they.

Nobody is perfect; this word confuses us because we like to believe things can be perfect, and with that belief comes unrealistic expectations of perfection. When things go bad, wrong, or just in an unexpected direction, we get stressed and wish for a perfect life; a life with no stress, just happiness. What we miss is that a happy life doesn't come with zero effort. For example, a great marriage doesn't just happen. If you think that your marriage is perfect and stop doing what you've been doing to get to that point, it will fall apart. To maintain perfection involves constant work and adaptation to change.

Nobody is perfect; however, a close second is to understand our own imperfections as well as the imperfections of others, while constantly striving for positive change. If you can master empathy, you will be on the right track to that place called Perfect.

END

57. MAKING IT BETTER

By Cheryl Vanbuuren

I opened my eyes and looked around…
The face of an angel is what I found.
Soon in the beginning of my brand new life,
I would call this angel mom, my daddy's wife.

The days flew by and soon I was seven.
This home in which I lived had to be just like heaven.
Warmth and love is what ran through our veins.
Understanding and kindness took away our pains.

Then on one quiet dark and dreary day,
The angel of my life was taken away.
I drew what strength I could from my dad.
But he was so awfully, terribly sad.

The house in which I lived had turned upside down.
My dad acted strange and wore a frown.
Cook and clean and earn some money.
How my brothers and I are wishing for mommy.

Now there was fear and no understanding.
What was wrong with dad who fell down to the landing?
Every day we would come home from a hard day at school.
Watch our father turn into a drunken fool.

Our friends want to come and play with us...
But dad would be drunk and yell and cuss.
I miss the love that we once shared.
I feel so lonely and I know he once cared.

He came out of the stupor once, no twice.
The future looked brighter and ever so nice.
But then it started all over again...
Now all I have is his picture in a frame.

I wish for the love like "Little House on the Prairie"
Or even my very own special blue fairy.
To grant me my wish of a mom and a dad.
And not leave me feeling rejected and sad.

I found what I thought was true love.
But soon realized that push came to shove.
Then came that look and familiar smell.
Just before he tripped and then fell.

Still I cook and clean and earn some money
But now my babies call me mommy.
Fear I once had buried deep in the past,
Was starting to seep out really fast.

I am not sure what hurt the most,
The punch in the face or the girls there to host.
The fear in their eyes broke my heart.
I knew my life was falling apart.

To die would have made all the pains go away.
But my girls they need me in every way.
They need the warmth and love in their veins,
Understanding and kindness to take away their pains.

204

So I tell him one day enough is enough,
Go and pack up all your meager stuff.
Out he walks with all the hurt and pain.
Now I can pick up and start my life again.

It may only be just the three of us,
But we have lots of love and other stuff.
We have a bond that is very strong.
It keeps us going from dusk until dawn.

58. LOVE ME WITH ALL OF YOUR HEART OR LEAVE ME WITH ALL OF MINE

Some of what you have read in this book may pertain to you, or perhaps to your ex. Sometimes when we read individual chapters we lose sight of the book's overall message and meaning; let's put it all together now.

At the very beginning, a relationship has gone sour. Boredom and frustration have set in. There is no communication and in time you drift apart. Every day is stressful, every day is an argument, and every day you hate your life. After torturing yourselves, the break-up comes. When the break-up comes, there are already feelings of hate, but now it is worse because each side feels that they are in the right, even though they are both guilty of not making the relationship work. Then comes the "I will change bit," and perhaps some relationships are saved right here...if not, you proceed to the next step.

You will go through the stages of grief, but you won't know why you are angry, jealous, or doing things you wouldn't normally do. It is difficult to go through these stages and deal with loss if you don't understand it and don't have friends and family to support you.

Just as a child will seek other role models, we will do the same and seek someone who makes us feel good. Anger increases with each minute of every day. It has now become a power struggle. Things you never thought you would hate or be upset about start coming out of nowhere. Things like a television, or a vehicle. When material things are over and done with, how can you continue punishing your partner? With what matters most, the kids. Getting the child to hate them will be the ultimate victory. "She got my car so I'll get our child to hate Mom," or "he never cared and now he will when his kids hate him."

Now others join in. Grandparents and friends add to the problem, expanding the abuse to the child, so now there is a whole gang of people hurting the child. This fuels the anger and the motivation to punish the ex; ultimately punishing the child, but this gets over-looked at this point. Things start coming out, like religion, fighting continues with an argument about going to church or not going to church. The religious side starts arguing that they are God's people, but they start doing bad things. They start abusing the child, by getting them to hate the other parent's house or religion.

Hate takes over and you can't tell the difference between love and hate. Then you forget about the truth and tell your child your personal views and perceptions about their other parent in the heat of anger. You are stressed out and don't see what you're doing to your child, even though you think it's right. Your anger keeps telling you that you are right, and it makes you feel better, so it must be right.

Now you're hiring lawyers and the hate doubles. Now you are paying ridiculous amounts of money, money you don't have, and things get tight. Groceries are a thing of the past and your anger toward your ex grows.

You think to yourself, what doesn't kill you makes you stronger, not a great motivational tool if you don't actually learn from it. You're not stronger at all; you're continuing to get angrier.

Even though you don't see it, your children are punished by your stress, no matter how well you think you are hiding it. Your thoughts don't stray from your hatred; now that it's started you must finish it. Unwilling to accept any other point of view, and no longer able to think for yourself, you become a moth at a window, a button pusher. It is unclear what your motivation is; love and hate have become confused.

The negative thoughts keep pouring in as you keep that door open, fuelling more unseen abuse to your child and yourself. To make things worse, your ex now has a new partner, taking the anger to a whole new level. The stepparent joins in the fight, just as the grandparents did, and now the war just got bigger. At this point, everyone is ignoring the child and not hearing their cries for help. Not seeing their innocence, playing, and wanting to have fun and be loved. You are breeding them to hate; this should be of no shock to you, as this is what you're teaching them. You hear from your lawyer the phrase, "in your child's best interests," but you don't really know what that means. You continue on your warpath, putting it in front of everything else. You say things like, "It's in my child's best interest to not ever see their other parent again."

Everything is stressful, even though you can't see it. If you didn't enjoy your work, now you hate it; everything contributes to your stress. If you smoke, you smoke more; if you drink, you drink more; if you eat unhealthy foods already, you now have less time to cook and you make yourself unhealthier. You feel worse and direct that anger, not at yourself, but at your ex. You don't fix the problem; you just shuffle it around like rotating the problematic tire, waiting for it to come around again.

You get so caught up in your anger that you don't see that you are viciously abusing your own child. You will forget all of this when time moves on; things will blow over, you will move on and be happy again. What is left behind though, is a child that has been changed, and years later you won't know why they're quiet, depressed, angry, violent; or why they ended up dead.

Let's look at the kid's point of view:

As the parents fight, the child gets ignored, not necessarily intentionally but because you are occupied with "adult stresses."

Your child's brain is developing, and everything taught to them will contribute to their development. A child needs love and attention, without it their brain will be undeveloped in those areas, leaving them challenged to find those feelings because their brain hasn't been programmed correctly.

A child will also feel ignored. Their huge accomplishments, for which they need validation and praise for go unnoticed. Something simple, such as playing with their toys, or building towers, is huge to them; we just see them as child's play. When that goes unnoticed, like adults without praise or a pat on the back for a job well done, children feel just as ignored and discouraged.

Instead of learning how to be social with a tea party, or playing with building blocks, they learn something we don't realize we're teaching them; to be cold, and turn to hate and anger easily. Fighting with another child is huge to them, just as it is to adults when they fight with others. What do parents do though? They see the fight between the kids as a simple fix. They either, separate the toys and tell them to share, or they redirect them outside or for an ice cream and things are okay. Why do adults not practice this? If they do, are things really ok?

A child being ignored will find other role models; just as we found a new partner that makes us feel good. Can we blame them? We do the same thing.

They become a moth at a window not being able to think for themselves, leaving their own negativity door open. Soon they don't have a button for anything. They grow up and show signs of depression, anger, and suicidal thoughts, or maybe they're overly quiet, shy, not able to be in public places. Anxiety gets the better of them. Maybe they are easily talked into uncomfortable situations because they lack self-esteem. They won't know why they are this way, and the parents accept no blame because they are unaware of the role they played. They are unaware because no one told them that what was happening to their child was bad.

If emotional abuse were as apparent as bruises from physical abuse, maybe more drastic measures would be taken. Just as it's easier to be negative than positive, it's hard to believe in something we cannot see, such as emotional abuse. We overlook the severity of it until the child is older and is a quiet, depressed or violent, and then we wash our hands of it. "Kids these days," we say, completely overlooking the emotional abuse from years ago as a possibility.

A child who has had a parent taken from them by Parent Alienation, a parent leaving, or a parent ignoring them, experiences a loss. Unfortunately, for the child, the parents do not see this as a loss for them as they didn't see their own loss when their relationship ended. As the parent experienced loss, and went through the stages of grief with the all-important love, support, and understanding of family and friends, a child was left alone during these stages of. They are forced to deal with the stages that even adults can be unaware of and have difficulty understanding. How could a child possibly do that alone?

The child turns into a teen, a teen into an adult, an adult into a parent, a parent into a grandparent and the cycle continues. It is time to stop this cycle.

So How Do We Stop This Cycle?

We start by remembering our own childhoods, remembering what it was like to be a kid. Remembering and talking about it may bring out some memories that you, yourself, have blocked. That's what counselors do. We must fix ourselves before we can expect to be able to fix others. We need to stop rotating our tires/problems and get to fixing them.

We must see the stages of grief and understand them as we go through them. With support, we as adults will eventually get to that acceptance stage where we can reflect with a clearer mind. What if no one sees or cares that you are going through these stages, what if you had no support? When a child deals with a loss and goes through these stages, we, as parents, are too involved in our own stresses to see it. If the only support a child has (the parents) isn't there to help them to the acceptance stage, do they ever get there? By the time parents, see the stages of grief in their children it's too late. The parents have moved on, and wonder why their children are displaying emotions such as:

Denial – nothing is wrong with them.

Anger – fighting in school, no respect.

Bargaining – maybe if they act differently, the situation will change.

Depression – suicide hotlines swamped with calls.

Acceptance – will they ever get to this stage?

These are all signs of children going through these stages, but unfortunately, many parents overlook them. We must recognize these signs and help them reach the acceptance stage before they become a statistic, a label, or a parent who teaches their kids the same thing without even knowing it.

In that time, we must be mindful of our children and how our actions and words affect them. We need to understand that all kids are different - there are no bad kids. There are simply kids who have different needs and perhaps have louder cries for help than others have. We must see that cries for help do not always come in the form of a direct question, or a letter asking for help. Sometimes, cries for help come in many different forms, some of which we may not see, such as being overly quiet or distant, or even angry and violent. Sometimes cries for help are what make parents, teachers, caregivers, family, and friends push them farther away. To understand this clearly, we MUST look into the works of Dr. Gordon Neufeld.

We must start seeing other options, and try hard to put ourselves in someone else's position, to see things from their point of view. It will help to make sense of things that you think make no sense at all. We must learn that empathy is a must.

We must remember that stress was so pre-2010 and it's time to be happier. To do this we must minimize our stress levels, and release the stress that comes our way. We must try to keep our stress vaults from filling up and being pushed to a forced release. We must realize this in our relationships, as talking about the things that bother us will keep the relationship going. Sometimes we don't talk to our partners about the things that upset us because we think they might be petty, or embarrassing to admit to. Things like being a little jealous and getting upset when your partner talked to someone else with a smile, or perhaps they smother ketchup all over the steak that you marinated to perfection and it bugged you. No matter how small it may seem, if it bugs you, tell them, let it out. It is the build-up of these small things that will eventually become fatal to your relationship. It's these small things that, if talked about, will be just that, small things, small things that are now dealt with and gone.

We also need to become healthier. Good health can help with depression. You will see life differently, get out from under that depressive cloud and feel good about pushing yourself to get there, to be healthy. We need to become more positive and laugh more. We need to choose not to be a button pusher or a moth at a window. We need to learn too, that we can do many things with lemons when life throws them our way.

We need to understand what abuse is, from yelling to teaching them to hate, and stop it now. We need to see that money isn't more important than our children are.

Like the sunflower, we must start believing in the things we cannot see and understand that they could be right in front of us. We must not think like the moth at my window, rather, we should start seeing these things, as well as opportunities for change and positive motivation, whatever that means to us. We need to understand that if something doesn't kill us, it doesn't automatically make us stronger. We must learn from that experience and seek education to keep it from happening again, that is what will make us stronger.

We must understand that changes don't happen overnight. We need to look at the end result of positive change, but not expect to get there instantly. We need to take baby steps, not being discouraged if progress is slow. You will get there eventually, and be proud of what you have accomplished.

Most importantly, whomever it is that you love, be it friend or family, love them with all of your heart, or leave them with all of theirs.

It's hard to believe in things we cannot see. It's difficult to keep a constant, and positive faith in the idea that good things are coming. It is not impossible, however, to do these things, and enjoy the benefits.

Emotional abuse is something we don't see until its effects show us how malicious it is. By then we have forgotten what got our children and us there.

When we can see the unseen and take the baby steps needed to correct it, then and only then, will we be able to break the cycle and move on into true happiness. After all, when our kids are happy, we are happy, right? And that kid is still within each of us; let's make them happy too.

If you are an alienating parent, and believe that nothing in this cycle resembles you in any way and you cannot relate to any of it; if the stages of grief were a breeze and you sailed the whole way through being mindful of your children's best interests; if your life growing up was perfect, you were given everything as a child, and there was zero possibility of being emotionally hurt by your parents; if you haven't been affected by any personal relationships that may have made you upset, and you don't feel that they were a loss of some sort; if you haven't been affected by something in your whole life that has made you angry, then please proceed to the first step.

First Step:

The first step is a slow and delicate process done with the adult's best interests in mind. A psychologist or counselor must go into the brain of the adult, with the careful intention to find the first underlying brick, which started the whole foundation. This emotionally sensitive process is much like peeling back the frail petals of a wilted rose, with the goal of reaching the un-damaged bud at the center and turning it, once again, into a beautiful flower.

EPILOGUE

I googled "cool as a cucumber" and found out that the cucumber is great for the skin. Its cooling effect does wonders for skin problems, and the cleansing action of the cucumber leaves your face soft and supple. Did you know also that a wild cucumber is known as "Man Root" and has a bitter taste?

To have healthy glowing skin, use this recipe I found by Sharon Hopkins:

Blend 4-5 leaves of fresh mint
Peel and deseed the cucumber
Add mint leaves to the cucumber and make a puree
Beat an egg white and keep it separate, then add this egg white to the cucumber mixture
Apply this evenly to your face for 20-30 minutes and rinse with tepid water and pat dry.

I'm not going to lie; before I could include this recipe in my book, I had to try it in case it melted your face and I got sued. I must say, with all of my testosterone left at the door, this was very refreshing. Just walking around with it on is like skiing down a mountaintop with the fresh mountain air gently caressing your face. Take that fresh mountain air and marinate in a bowl of refreshing mint, add some eye firming egg whites and a splash of mmmm...Ahem.

My point is this:

If you are a father, it is great to show your child man stuff; however, don't be afraid to show your child a softer side, a side that might be lacking without Mom being there. It is important for a child to have both parents, and if they can't have that, be mindful of fulfilling all of your child's needs.

I have been a single father for thirteen years and have realized that I can't only teach my son "man stuff," such as calling our house The Man Pad, or The Ken Den all the time. He needs a softer side as well, so I buy fresh flowers for our table even if he thinks it's weird, and I did indeed try the cucumber facial. The funniest part about doing the facial was that my younger son's mom busted me when she dropped him off an hour early. I was cleaning the house sporting my lovely, manly cucumber facial and saw an instant change, or sigh of relief, in her. She saw that it wasn't always just "guy stuff" at Dad's house. That we did things like every "normal family" would do with a mom around. She was more at ease knowing that. This goes both ways, so parents: always be mindful of your child in every way and be less mindful of the anger you have toward your ex.

I also went back to the arcade with my son. This time there was no stress or pressure to win the sticky hand, just fun. I returned to the creepy broken doll and again it would not dance. This time was different however, without the stress I just looked at it.

I felt for that weird doll and started to realize why it didn't work, why it had stopped dancing. If everybody pushed a button and expected us to dance, we would do the same. Perhaps the worker at the fast food place visited the same arcade and got a little carried away with the non-button pushing, I don't know. What I do know is this:

We are not puppets made to dance at the push of a button; we are our own loving and capable selves. I learned not to dance when negativity says dance, why should it have that power? It doesn't.

We all know what is good and bad, right and wrong. Even so, negativity, the Puppet Master, pulls our strings, pushes our buttons and makes us dance. It is not a waltz or the club kind of dance, it is one of stress. Stress that clouds us, makes us unsure, makes us doubt ourselves. This dance will destroy us eventually, as the Puppet Master makes us dance into a world of stress. It may be by way of nicotine, alcohol or drug use, and it may be by way of emotionally abusing our own children for the sake of revenge.

I once laughed at the old doll in the arcade, but it taught me a lesson. We are not puppets, negativity and emotional abuse cannot pull our strings and make us dance. We can stand up and say no. It may be difficult and we may be like the weird doll who didn't dance, but we will be just that, the doll that didn't dance - embrace that. When I embraced it, I wrote another letter, this time it wasn't to stress, it was to emotional abuse. It was titled "Love Me With All Of Your Heart Or Leave Me With All Of Mine."

REFERENCES:

Burrill, Gerald. Referenced (2011) on www.quotesdaddy.com.

Foisy, Sue. Transitions Facilitator. The Bridge Youth And Family Services, Kelowna, BC.

Gorkin, Mark. 2004. *Practice Safe Stress.* First Books Library.

Kübler Ross, Dr. Elisabeth. 1969. *On Death and Dying.* Simon & Schuster: A Touchstone Book.

Schwarzenegger, Arnold. 1987. *Encyclopedia Of Modern Bodybuilding.* Simon & Schuster

Simon, Dr. Sidney. 1990. *I Am Loveable and Capable: A Modern Allegory on the Classical Put-Down.* Values Pr.

Warshak, Dr. Richard A. 2010. *Divorce Poison.* New York: HarperCollins Publishers Inc.

Websites (2011):
    www.google.com
    www.wikipedia.com
    www.divorcesource.com
    www.parentalalienationawareness.com
    www.hubpages.com

Songs & Other Artists:
    "Why I Oughta's", by the Three Stooges.
    "47 Beavers On The Big Blue Sea" written by Phil Vischer.
    "You Can't Be A Beacon" written By Martin Cooper.
    "Man in Black" written by Johnny Cash.
    "The Gambler" written by Don Schlitz.

CPSIA information can be obtained at www.ICGtesting.com
Printed in the USA
LVOW061131130312

272723LV00023B/2/P